SOUGHT THROUGH
MEDITATION

Buddhism & the Twelve Steps

SOUGHT THROUGH MEDITATION

Exploring the Eleventh Step through the Lens of Dharma

By Kevin Griffin

ONE BREATH BOOKS

Buddhism & the Twelve Steps: SOUGHT THROUGH MEDITATION

Copyright 2024 by Kevin Griffin

All rights reserved. No part of this publication may be reproduced or transmitted in any form or by any means, electronic or mechanical, including photocopying, recording, or any other information storage and retrieval system without written permission of the publisher.

Cover painting adapted from photo by Greg Pergament.

First Edition, September 2024

One Breath Books

ISBN 978-0-9996789-3-0

Table of Contents

Preface	9
Part I: Step Eleven	13
Introduction	14
Bill's Eleventh Step	15
The Step	19
My Story	24
Part II: Buddhist Meditation	45
The Background	46
Practice	48
How to Meditate	51
The Basics	51
The Details	51
How It Works	54
More on Mindfulness	55
Mindfulness with Breathing	59
More on Concentration	61
Challenges to Practice	64
The Five Hindrances	65
Working with Thoughts	70
Changing Our Relationship to Difficult Emotions	73
Working with Physical Pain	75
Meditation and the Twelve Steps	78
Heart Practices	94
Part III: The Whole of Our Lives	103
Insight and Spiritual Awakening	104
Teachers and Community	108
Retreats	111
Daily Practice	114
Part IV: Guided Meditations	119

Getting Started	*120*
Standard Mindfulness Practice	*120*
Noting	*121*
Sweeping	*122*
Anapanasati – Mindfulness with Breathing	*123*
Gathas	*126*
Counting Breaths	*127*
Metta – Phrases	*128*
Metta – Images	*130*
Forgiveness	*132*
Other Practices	*134*
Appendix I: Buddhist Lists	*135*
Appendix II: The Twelve Steps of Alcoholics Anonymous	*138*
Appendix III: Buddhist Traditions	*139*
Resources	*141*
Acknowledgments	*144*

Step Eleven

"Sought through prayer and meditation to improve our conscious contact with God, as we understood Him, praying only for knowledge of His will for us and the power to carry it out."

Preface

This is the shortest of my books. That's not because I don't have a lot to say about meditation, but because I wanted to get to the heart of things and trim away any of the extras. Here, I am offering you the essence of my understanding of mindfulness meditation, the heart of Buddhist practice, framed within the Twelve Step context. No doubt, this is a complicated topic, but at the end of the day, the most important thing is to do it, to sit, to practice. If you use this book to learn to meditate, I have no doubt that you will be curious to read more, to hear other teachers, to go deeper with your practice. At the same time, I believe that you will find enough in these pages to carry you a long way.

While I can give you a lot of important information in this book, if you are serious about meditation, you will want to do it with others. Just as with recovery, establishing and sustaining a meditation practice alone is difficult. If there is a group or teacher near you, join them. If not, you may have to travel. Go for a retreat for a day or longer. Try different teachers. Meet people and build a community of like-minded folks. Mindfulness meditation is more than an activity to fit into your day. It is a way of living in the world. I hope you will take hold and let the practice carry you deeper into your life.

June, 1985

It's my first AA meeting. It's not my first day sober. That was a couple weeks ago. I wasn't ready to jump into this whole program thing. I'm not a joiner. Never even was a cub scout. But it feels almost superstitious to be here, like I better do this or maybe I'll drink. Even though I have no desire. That just disappeared when I woke up that day. Weird, but I know it's over.

This meeting is called "Monday Night Venice" even though it's a couple blocks south in Santa Monica. I guess you can't expect a bunch of alcoholics to be great with geography.

When they ask for "newcomers" to raise their hands, I don't. I really don't want the attention, all the clapping and staring and people giving you their phone number. As if I'd ever call one of these people. I just keep my head down. I'm not here to make friends.

In the front of the room are hanging a couple of scrolls. One says, "Twelve Traditions" and the other "Twelve Steps." So that's the famous Twelve Steps. I begin to read them...powerless, God, inventory, I don't know what they're talking about. Until I get to eleven: meditation. That's something I know about...

Part I: Step Eleven

Introduction

Although meditation appears as a part of Step Eleven of the Twelve Steps, when I got sober in 1985, it was the prayer portion of the Step that got most of the attention. Twelve Step meetings usually included the Serenity Prayer and/or the Lord's Prayer ("Our Father"), while few included periods of meditation. I came to recovery with a fairly extensive background in meditation, so my approach was always different. And now, after thirty-nine years sober (and counting), and almost thirty as a meditation teacher, my recovery program doesn't look much like the traditional one, nor, in fact, like my early days of sobriety.

I've written a series of books that are meant to help people use Buddhist teachings and practices as a foundation for their Twelve Step work. All of them talk about meditation. This one takes that as its sole topic.

The word meditation has always had a mysterious quality to it, as though there were some magical experience waiting for us or superpowers we might unlock. But meditation isn't a way to escape the world or control it. It is, in fact, a deep engagement with reality just as it is, and a profound letting go.

Many people struggle to establish a meditation practice. They understand that meditation isn't a one-off, but something that depends on consistency and showing up, just like recovery. If you have been able to establish that steadiness in your recovery, perhaps ask yourself what you draw on to accomplish that. Then see if you can apply those same skills or tools to a meditation practice.

I would argue that what inspires recovery is our experience of the suffering our addiction caused us and others. The pain of that experience motivates us to do the difficult work of recovery, and to keep doing it. I believe that if you look deeply into your heart and mind, you can find the same kind of inspiration to meditate. What you find there, as the Buddha pointed out, are "greed, hatred, and delusion," or less dramatically, a craving for things to be different from the way they are and a repeated effort to control things beyond your control. When you see this inner struggle, this "dukkha," as the Buddha calls it, you can't help but yearn for a way out, a way to let go. And that's what meditation offers.

While some people struggle to establish this discipline, others find that once they engage in the process they feel frustrated by their own busy minds. How often has someone said to me, "I think too much," or "I have a really noisy head," or some such comment? They seem to think that they are unique—a common fallacy among addicts, as we know. The truth is, they are simply encountering the human condition. Thinking, and thinking more or less constantly, is a habit tied deeply into our evolution as human beings. It is our intelligence, our ability to remember and to problem-solve that sets us apart—and above—the other organisms on our planet. To stop thinking, then, feels dangerous, like a threat to our safety. Thinking is what protects me from danger. If I stop, won't I be opening myself to danger? This is our subconscious belief, often unseen, unacknowledged, and unchallenged. When we start to meditate we don't get a direct message that it's dangerous, but rather a flood of thoughts our subconscious throws up to protect us. The first challenge of meditation is to navigate this flood and learn to let it pass without getting agitated.

And so, like recovery, meditation depends on showing up,

just doing it, overcoming all the resistance and all the stories that tell us we can't do it, or now isn't the right time, or there must be an "easier, softer way." I encourage you to begin and to continue. That's all that's needed. Great things will come from those simple acts.

Warning: Meditation is not a recovery program. It is an invaluable part of a program, but more is needed. We need self-examination, admission of defeat, support of others, and much more. Twelve Step programs offer these tools, as do various Buddhist recovery programs. Trying to maintain sobriety alone or meditate our way out of our problems is rarely successful. I hope that you will pick up meditation as one of your many tools for recovery.

Please note: I do not endorse the masculine pronoun in Step Eleven or the other Steps. However, I prefer not to put the Steps into different language because once you open that door the fixes could be endless. Nonetheless, I affirm that I don't believe that God is a man—or for that matter, that God has gender. (Defining God is another question altogether, one I address in my book *Buddhism & the Twelve Steps: HIGHER POWER.*)

Bill's Eleventh Step

The writings of Bill Wilson, the co-founder of AA, are the foundational texts of AA, and as such are an excellent starting point in contrasting Buddhist meditation with a Twelve Step approach. The chapter on Step Eleven in his book, Twelve Steps and Twelve Traditions, better known as the "12 x 12," (pronounced "twelve and twelve") expands on what he already wrote in the Big Book. When I reread it recently, what surprised me was how much it focuses on God. Here is where the Twelve Steps clearly diverge from Buddhism, a non-theistic religion.

I shouldn't be surprised. After all, the Step itself says that the purpose of our meditation is to get closer to God, figure out what He wants us to do, and develop the capacity to carry out that guidance. In the "12 x 12," instead of suggesting anything a Buddhist would call meditation, he suggests thoughtfully going through the St. Francis Prayer. As a technique this might be closest to something like chanting a sutta or reflecting on compassion. Buddhist practices begin with what's called "mind training," cultivating mindfulness and concentration. Reflecting on or reciting a prayer in a disciplined way can actually help develop such qualities, but without explicit instruction in that direction, one can easily miss this aspect of prayer. Bill doesn't seem to have known anything about these important aspects of meditation. That means we're expected to navigate this tricky territory ourselves, which is one reason so many people in Twelve Step programs struggle to develop a meditation practice.

Standard aspects of Buddhist meditation like posture, breath, noticing thoughts, working with sensations, sleepiness, restlessness, none of this is found in Bill's writing. That's one of the main reasons why I embarked on this work over twenty years ago.

Having read a bit about Bill's life and spiritual journey, I become even more mystified why his understanding—or at least written understanding—of meditation didn't seem to evolve. While it's known that he experimented with LSD in the 1950s, we also see him writing about meditation in the AA Grapevine in June 1958 with thoughts that could have been lifted from his writing of twenty years before. Here he repeats ideas that for non-theists can only be described as patronizing, and today actually seem silly. We're supposed to believe that if we just try hard enough to pray, we'll end up believing in God. Those of us who don't are just stubborn cynics according to him.

Unless you get the wrong impression, I want you to know that I have incredible gratitude and respect for Bill. Without him, I and millions of others would probably never have gotten sober. His work developing and writing about the program is some of the most important spiritual work of the 20th century. But all that doesn't mean I can't take issue with some of his thinking.

Obviously Bill came from a certain religious and cultural background—Protestant, New England, white, educated—that colored his way of understanding religious and spiritual ideas. He wasn't exposed to the Buddhism that I first encountered in 1980. These teachings don't concern themselves with God, creation, or petitionary prayer. The Buddha's focus was "suffering and the end of suffering." He often left the "Big Questions" unanswered, seeing them as distractions from his core work. Sure, it's interesting to ponder how the universe began, but does that really help you here and now? (Bill actually expresses similar sentiments in the Big Book.) By zeroing in on the state of body and mind we brush aside anything that hinders our progress toward freedom from inner turmoil and angst.

Of course, Bill wants the same thing—freedom from suffering. He just approaches that work differently. It's interesting, though, that in that Grapevine piece he seems to be expressing his own sense of not really getting it, not achieving serenity, not establishing a fulfilling meditation practice. He talks about other people and how they've achieved great things, but his own reflection seems to be on his shortcomings. That might just be humility, but it reads more as confession. I can only think that Bill would have found great solace had he ever been exposed to Buddhist meditation, or picked it up in a serious way.

Let's talk, though, about his suggestion to use the St. Francis Prayer in meditation. Its theme is service. One seeks to dispel destructive forces through offering their opposite: to hatred bring love, to discord bring harmony, to doubt bring faith. All the principles expressed here fit with Buddhism, sometimes explicitly, other times more generally. What it is doing is laying out a set of goals, of intentions to align ourselves with "God's will," or in Buddhist terms, with the Law of Karma. The final line, "It is by dying that one awakens to eternal life," can be understood to refer to ego death—simply put, not thinking about yourself all the time—
and living fully in the eternal present moment.

All of this is beautiful and inspiring. For me, though, I need more than words. Reading this prayer can uplift me for a moment or a few minutes, but without some practice, without addressing all the forces that pull me toward the negative, destructive forces, the best of intentions pretty quickly slip away. Buddhist practice is meant to both inspire and give you a reference point, a grounding in something that you can call on to pull yourself out of that destructiveness in a moment: mindfulness. By meditating on the breath regularly you develop new habits that tend toward being awake, conscious. An actual transformation happens—a spiritual awakening, if you will—that doesn't depend upon momentary inspiration and reflection, but becomes more deeply ingrained in the psyche and even in the body. This is the difference between the results of a meditation practice and a simple prayer.

Now, I recognize that I'm biased in this regard. No doubt serious practitioners of prayer can also create a psychic change, but I would argue that such a practice becomes more and more like a meditation practice, and less like a petition to a Higher Power to fix you, as so many prayers sound.

There is a great deal of wisdom in Bill's words. When he emphasizes St. Francis's plea for "self-forgetting," he's aligning with the idea of "not-self" which is key to Buddhist insight. He tells us that meditation "can always be further developed," that it is without boundaries. These ideas sound like the immeasurable and formless qualities that describe Buddhist meditation. But then he falls back on the idea that it's all about "improving conscious contact with God." There he loses me. Maybe that's my lack of imagination, but it just feels as if he's trying to lure us into a Christian, devotional, faith-based process rather than the more open-ended search for Truth that the Dharma invites.

At the end of the day, I'm grateful that Bill intuited the need for meditation of some sort in the recovery program he helped shape. If his approach differs from mine, that's fine. He opened a door that I walked through—or maybe I found a second door after the first one. In any case, the invitation to meditate meant that for me, as at that first meeting, I felt an immediate connection to at least one aspect of the program. It also meant that all these years later I could begin to make these connections between Buddhism and the Twelve Steps that might never have been made without that critical inclusion in Step Eleven.

The Step

Compared to the Buddhist approach to meditation, Step Eleven sets forth fairly limited goals in meditation. It's a little difficult to understand from the Step itself what is expected, but it seems that improving "conscious contact" with God and "knowledge of His will" are the two purposes of the Step. What adds to the challenge of understanding this is that the Twelve Step literature seems to conflate prayer and meditation.

I've often been asked what "Buddhist prayer" is, or if there is such a thing. So now we are faced with defining terms. Although we can look to the dictionary for help here, what is most important is that we find practical ways to understand these ideas and create some kind of distinction between them.

First of all, prayer. The typical way of understanding prayer is as a plea to God for some result. We pray for success or healing or understanding. This type of prayer doesn't exactly apply in Buddhism because there is no God to pray to in Buddhism. Nonetheless, many Buddhist traditions have deities or Bodhisattvas that one might call upon, but their function isn't like the omnipotent creator-God of the Abrahamic tradition (Judaism, Christianity, and Islam which all view Abraham as a founder). Clearly what's implied in any of these forms is a belief that some external force or power can intervene in our lives. It's easy to see how such thinking can be counter-productive, taking away our own agency and responsibility and giving it to some invisible being. While this can certainly bring some degree of comfort, for many of us, such thinking simply isn't supportable. You don't have to be an atheist to think that this doesn't make much sense.

Does that mean that prayer has no value or use? Not at all. If we start by asking what is happening when we pray, I think we can make sense of this. When we pray, we are talking to ourselves, planting positive, constructive thoughts and intentions in our mind. Let's look at the Serenity Prayer:

"God, grant me the serenity to accept the things I cannot change, courage to change the things I can, and wisdom to know the difference."

Here we're being reminded to look at our thoughts and behavior and see if:

1) We are creating agitation in our mind by trying to control the uncontrollable. If so, we encourage ourselves to let go, to accept things as they are.

2) We are avoiding dealing with challenging issues. If so, we try to overcome our fear and act wisely.

3) We can distinguish between the things we control and those we don't. By focusing on this question, we are trying to bring more clarity to our decision-making.

In contrast, let's take a common Buddhist form, Loving-kindness meditation, or "Metta." In the Metta Sutta the Buddha suggests that one should think in this way: "wishing, in gladness and in safety, may all beings be at ease." Later in the same sutta he says, "radiating kindness over the entire world." "Wishing" seems a lot like praying. "Radiating" starts to move the wish into the realm of imagination, but still has the sense of a prayer. It's certainly not the kind of passive stillness one might associate with a Buddhist meditator (although this is a misunderstanding that I'll address later).

In Buddhist terms, what we are doing in both cases, the Serenity Prayer and Metta meditation, is "cultivating." We are trying to plant more helpful, wise, and loving thoughts and attitudes in our mind, and counteract the less helpful ones.

We aren't doing this by calling on some external force, but by intentionally looking at things differently, trying to view them through a different lens.

Notice, though, that I call Metta practice a "meditation." Now we can see that the question of meditation versus prayer is getting thornier. If we've gotten hold of the meaning of prayer, what, then, is meditation?

Before I even attempt to answer that question, I want to say that there simply is no one answer. Much of what I want to do with this book is to help you explore the various forms of practice, so I don't want to limit the idea of what meditation is. But let's start with the dictionary, Bill W., and the early Twelve Step literature.

In a Webster's dictionary from 1988, meditation is defined as "deep, continued thought," and "solemn reflection of sacred matters." This aligns with Bill Wilson's writing in the Twelve Steps and Twelve Traditions, where he suggests we reflect on the St. Francis Prayer as a meditation. We can also see in the Big Book of Alcoholic Anonymous that he's pointing toward the same orientation, asking that we spend time in the morning and evening reflecting on our day and seeking intuitive answers to pressing problems and issues in our lives.

In recent decades, mindfulness, Buddhism, and likely Transcendental Meditation (TM) have changed our understanding of the term meditation. Now an internet search shows Merriam-Webster's giving a traditional definition first, but then offering this: "to engage in mental exercise (such as concentration on one's breathing or repetition of a mantra) for the purpose of reaching a heightened level of spiritual awareness." This is much closer to what people mean today when they say "meditation." (As for defining "spiritual awareness," I refer you, again, to *Buddhism & the Twelve Steps: HIGHER POWER*)

My conclusion then is that while Buddhist practices have some overlap with the original and literal meaning of Step Eleven, they eventually take us to different places and essentially leave the Step behind. For me, these places expand on and deepen my life and spiritual practice in ways that the Twelve Steps and Twelve Step programs alone simply could not. That is for a simple reason: the primary purpose of all Twelve Step programs is to overcome addiction. Buddhism's primary purpose is more lofty: to overcome suffering. The obvious parallel is that addiction is one kind of suffering. What Buddhism does is help us to see and overcome more and more subtle forms of suffering.

Let me get back to the Step itself. The term "conscious contact" is a synonym for mindfulness. If we drop the God issues (admittedly a big ask), or make God a more general term for "reality," or "the present moment," then we land right on Buddhist practice. We are trying to be more present for our lives, to see things more objectively, to take things less personally. The effort to "improve" in this regard is essentially what mindfulness meditation and mindful activity is about. I'll spend much more time exploring mindfulness itself later, but for now, we can make this connection with Step Eleven: it's about becoming more mindful, more present, more awake for our lives.

Meditation also relates directly to growing intuition. In order to become more present, we have to let go of some of the persistent and intrusive thoughts that tend to fill the mind. As those thoughts recede, more clarity arises, and our thinking becomes less self-centered and more intuitive. We start to tune into the natural wisdom that we all carry within us. When we, again, take this out of the theistic language of the Step and think of it more organically, "knowledge of His will," becomes something like "clear thinking," or in Buddhist terms "clear comprehension." Our thinking is unobstructed by ego, bias, grasping, and aversion. With such clarity comes the capacity to act with confidence and persistence. We're not confused or emotionally distraught. Similar to how we become more functional when we stop drinking, using, or engaging in any addictive behavior, our ability to act improves as our addiction to thought and its accompanying grasping subsides. Now we become increasingly effective people. We have he "power to carry out" wise choices.

My Story

We're going to have to go back a ways, so bear with me. Or just skip ahead. Up to you.

It all starts with the Beatles. I was the perfect age to be under their influence. Fourteen when they appeared on Ed Sullivan, ready for "I Want to Hold Your Hand" and "She Loves You." Seventeen when Sergeant Pepper's Lonely Hearts Club Band came out, ready for "Lucy in the Sky with Diamonds," and "A Day in the Life." I started smoking pot that summer, 1967.

But it was their excursion into Transcendental Meditation (TM) that fascinated me. I imagined some bliss state, some magical transformation that would fix everything. That's what I thought meditation would be. Why didn't I try it then? Let me count the ways. By that time I had already dropped out of high school. I struggled with depression. I wanted to be a musician (again, blame the Beatles). Pretty quickly I descended into intense drug use and drinking. In my lucid moments I might still think about some kind of spiritual experience, but I simply didn't have the wherewithal to take the actions necessary.

Over the succeeding years I found a couple reasons not to study meditation, and specifically TM. First there was money. I was a starving musician; how could I come up with the small fee required? Soon, though, there was another impediment: I learned that you had to stop smoking marijuana for two weeks before they would teach you the technique. For many years this was an insurmountable obstacle. From age 19 to 28, I smoked pot daily—every single day, unless there was some crisis, like I ran out and couldn't find any. The idea of going a day without getting high was unimaginable. The couple days over those years when I ran out were torturous.

Looking back, it's quite amazing that I considered marijuana to be non-addictive. The idea that I was a drug addict would have horrified me. Rebellious, out of the mainstream, sure, but an "addict"? No way. But that is the power of denial, or as a Buddhist would say, ignorance (the misunderstanding of reality).

At 28 I was playing guitar in a remarkable band called Lofty's Zzebra, led by a Nigerian saxophonist and percussionist named Lofty Amao (Abdul Lassisi Amao was his given name). The band, based in Vermont, had a spiritual element to it, something magical and powerful, although that element was mixed with the usual hedonism of 1970's rock culture. Nonetheless, the lead singer and I started talking about learning TM. We visited the local center where we were informed that it would cost $150 to get our mantra. By now I understood that what TM involved was repeating a Sanskrit word or phrase that a TM teacher would give you. At the center we were told that this mantra would be specially adapted to us individually. If we practiced long and hard enough, we'd attain "cosmic consciousness." It all sounded appropriately magical and mystical. However, the fee was beyond my ability to pay. Zzebra was not raking it in. I was living in a Vermont farmhouse with three other band members, paying $35 a month rent.

Kindly, the TM folks gave me a discount and I signed up for the training. Now I just had to stop smoking pot for two weeks. As the Big Book says, "What an order, I can't go through with it." I was determined, though, so I quit.

I noticed right away that I had a lot more energy. Again, looking back, it's almost sad to realize that it didn't occur to me that this might be a good thing, that in fact, pot was sapping my energy. No. Instead I just drank more during those two weeks. Nothing in the TM handbook said anything about drinking, as far as I knew.

Finally the day came, and I went into a quiet room at the TM center with a slender, long-haired woman who was a few years older than me. She gave me my mantra. She told me how the first time she got her mantra she left the center feeling spaced out and kind of drifted home in bliss. For me, the experience was more anticlimactic. I just sat there, repeated the word and tried to focus. Most of the time my mind was wandering, but I was told that this wasn't a problem. Just, whenever you realized you weren't repeating the mantra, come back and start again.

It's clear to me now that my reluctance to give up drugs and alcohol and fully embrace spiritual principles limited my experience with TM. I soon returned to using marijuana, though I never became a daily smoker again. While my TM practice never went beyond a superficial level, what I certainly did get was discipline. I followed the instruction to meditate for twenty minutes twice a day religiously. This has held me in good stead.

Sidebar: Transcendental Meditation: TM is a Hindu-based style of meditation that uses a sacred word, or mantra, as a concentration device. These are Sanskrit words, the ancient ecclesiastical language of India to which special powers are sometimes attributed. The practice, as taught by Maharishi Mahesh Yogi, simply involved silently repeating the mantra for twenty-minutes. While the mantras are supposed to be assigned by some subtle analysis of the student's personality and proclivities, an article in Omni magazine in the early 1980s revealed that they were simply assigned by age.

And so, TM was my practice for two years. Sitting in a truck on the way to a gig, I repeated my mantra; in the back of the club after sound check, I repeated my mantra. Every morning and evening, I did my twenty minutes twice a day. Very little happened. But I did adopt a new identity: meditator. I started dating a woman who was doing Zen practice and started reading about Buddhism. After those two years Zzebra started to fall apart. We'd moved to LA by then and I was working in a health food store (part of my new "spiritual" identity). There, in the spring of 1980, I heard about a meditation teacher named Joseph Goldstein who taught "vipasanna," some kind of Buddhist meditation. The produce manager had been on a ten-day retreat with Joseph and others in Joshua Tree, and every time he had a break, we'd follow him out to the sidewalk where he'd regale us with tales of the magical experience of a silent meditation retreat. It sounded incredible. And undoable. If quitting pot for two weeks had been hard, what about ten days of silent meditation?

Nonetheless, I got a copy of Joseph's book, The Experience of Insight, which was adapted from talks given on a thirty-day retreat (!). The book was a revelation. It laid out Buddhist teachings in easy-to-understand instructions, stories, and explanations of the foundation principles. I felt myself being pulled onto this path. That fall, after one last trip to Vermont for some final gigs with Zzebra before leaving the band, my girlfriend and I found a monk at the International Buddhist Meditation Center in LA who was offering a weekly class on vipassana. Recently returned from eight years in Sri Lanka, this monk—Akasa—was more casual than I expected. On Wednesday evenings we'd show up for the class and he would put a cassette player on the floor of the meditation hall. A recording of Stephen Levine (another rising Buddhist teacher) giving meditation instructions would start, and Akasa would leave the hall. Afterward he'd come back and take questions or give a talk.

It was there that I first tried to sit cross-legged. There were zafus in the hall—the hard, round Japanese meditation cushions. And I would sit in a version of lotus posture. After fifteen or twenty minutes my knees would start to hurt; then burn; then kill me. Finally I would move. The sits were forty-five minutes, and I probably never actually sat still for an entire period.

Now I wasn't using a mantra, but was learning to pay attention to the breath.

The technique we were learning seems to have been developed in Burma. It involved something called "noting." Here, you started with attention to the breath, silently noting, "In, out," with the movement of the breath. Then, if your mind wandered, you noted "thinking, thinking." You could note thoughts more precisely: "planning, planning," or "judging, judging," and so on. You could also note "hearing, hearing," or "feeling, feeling." I liked this practice because, as with mantra, it gave my mind something to do. But, other than the relief of the bell ringing at the end of forty-five minutes, not much seemed to be happening.

Here I think I should talk about faith. What was it that kept me meditating for those years, every day, when I couldn't really detect anything happening? I had lots of ideas about how I was supposed to feel, but what I experienced was mostly frustration. However, there was always a part of me that believed it was worth it. Part of this was magical thinking: I thought that even if I couldn't feel it, some "karma" was accumulating and at some point everything would pop. Enlightenment would happen. Whatever that was. Whether this was delusional or not, it served me well. It kept me going until (as you will learn) something did actually start to happen.

Besides faith, I also had (and have) a personality that likes routine. Without going too far into my past, I can safely say that this came from my father, who lived a life of routines. So much so that, as with many children, I wanted to live the opposite life, which is part of why I chose to be a musician, a life that is often defined by chaos. But, again, as with many of us, despite my best efforts to be different from my father, in my own way I replicated his behavior. And so, meditating in a very disciplined way evolved quite naturally.

Sidebar: Vipassana: The term "vipassana" means to "see clearly" or "insight," and has been applied to the style of meditation taught in the Theravada Buddhist tradition, found primarily in Thailand, Burma (Myanmar), and Sri Lanka. While the Buddha didn't teach vipassana, per se, he used the term to describe the meditation practices that we now refer to as "mindfulness." The Indian meditation teacher S.N. Goenka, who learned the practice in Burma, laid claim to the term, which may be one of the reasons that Western Buddhists now prefer the English term "insight" to describe their own version of vipassana. Goenka's version of vipassana is a more regimented and narrowly-defined set of practices, while the Western Insight tradition draws from a broader range of sources and practices.

Through the fall of 1980 I soldiered on, trying to get a grip on vipassana meditation. As I did so, and as I read Joseph's book, I couldn't avoid the fact that retreats seemed to be a critical piece of this practice. Soon we learned that Akasa was going to offer a five-day session in Joshua Tree over Thanksgiving Weekend. My girlfriend signed up, and she and Akasa began to work on me. I was scared.

What was going to happen? If forty-five minutes of meditation was painful, what would five days be like? And silence? How would I handle that?

A couple more things about my personality come into play here. First of all, I'm not a joiner. (It's something of a miracle that I ever joined a Twelve Step program.) So being part of a group retreat felt alien. Secondly, I have a history of depression, and if there's one thing that causes problems for a depressive it's being alone with your own thoughts. Now, technically, on a retreat you aren't alone, but in practical terms, you are. You're sitting, walking, eating, and doing every other activity with no distraction, no conversation, nothing to take your mind off yourself. I have to admit that, to this day—over forty years later—I still have some trepidation about this when approaching a retreat.

Despite all this, I really wanted to go on the retreat. I had convinced myself that five days of meditation would change everything. I would finally "get it," the peace and bliss of meditation; my knees would no longer hurt; I would step over the threshold into a transcendent spiritual state. So, I agreed to go.

And boy was I wrong.

Let me just say that I have read various people's descriptions of their first meditation retreat, and I think those stories have become somewhat cliched, so I'm not going to go into the particulars. Nothing very striking about it. The usual agitation, restlessness, boredom, and frustration. The long trains of thought. Strings of memories, fantasies, and judgments.

And afterward? Suffice it to say that, rather than returning home in a state of bliss, I found myself crying every day the following week. It turns out that rather than being at the end of some process, I was at the beginning. One friend told me that my heart was opening, and that's as good a description of what happened as anything. At thirty-years-old, I realized I probably hadn't cried since I was fifteen. It was bitter-sweet. And I was learning one of the prime lessons of the spiritual path: you don't get to control it.

Besides teaching vipassana, at the end of the retreat Akasa introduced us to loving kindness meditation, or metta. This is an essential Buddhist practice meant to bring more openness, compassion, and care and to provide a helpful balance to the drier aspects of strict vipassana.

Despite the challenges of that first retreat, what it did do was plunge me deeper onto the path. Even though my meditation still felt pretty shallow, some thing or things were happening. I remember going back home to Pennsylvania for Christmas and noticing, for the first time, the beauty of my hometown, the old houses, stately trees, and rolling hills of my childhood, things I had taken for granted. My newfound connection with mindfulness seemed to bring them alive for me now.

Another strange memory: I taught my mother to mediate on that visit. She was 71 years old and managed to kneel in seiza posture and follow my instructions. I don't remember much else about that experience, except that she had always associated me—her youngest son—with spirituality for some reason.

The next significant moment in my meditation journey happened on a Presidents' Day weekend retreat in February. This event took place at the International Buddhist Meditation Center itself where we more or less camped out in the Dharma hall. There are two memories that stand out: first, doing walking meditation in the garden behind the hall and having one of those ineffable moments that often arise on retreat, feeling so present, so connected with the earth, the air, the sky, the sunlight. Early in my practice, before I developed much concentration in my sitting meditation, these walking moments tended to be the most impactful. In sitting meditation, you might strain to concentrate and get caught in frustration with the wandering mind. Walking meditation tends to allow for more natural moments of presence and insight, as you are doing an ordinary activity with increased attention.

The second moment happened while sitting. The unheated hall was quite chilly and most of the large group was wrapped up in shawls and blankets on Sunday afternoon. I, on the other hand, was sweating in a light tee shirt. Presumably whatever effort I was making or whatever development was happening in my practice was manifesting as heat in my body. I didn't understand what was happening (I'm not sure I do now, for that matter), but I was impressed. Something was happening, at least, even if I didn't know what it was. At that point, I was grateful for any signs of progress, no matter how obscure.

Apparently my condition drew the attention of Akasa, who kindly came by and touched my shoulder in support as the sweat poured off my brow. Little moments like that mean a lot to the fledgling meditator. Now, though, my practice was about to move into a dramatically more intensive period.

Here, I want to pull back and say a couple things as well as make some other observations. First of all, I am writing all these details not as a personal memoir but in the hopes that reading about some of the patterns and processes I experienced will resonate for others on the path. One of the greatest challenges of spiritual practices is feeling alone, and especially feeling flawed. I hope that seeing the roller coaster of my journey will relieve my readers of some of their own self-judgments and doubt.

As for my own story, at this point it's worth noting that a short time before this immersion in Buddhist practice I had been immersed in a career as a musician. For a decade, the most important thing in my life had been trying to survive and find success as a guitarist and songwriter. Zzebra had seemed like the key to this success, and its dissolution had a traumatic impact on my life—a loss I still feel today. The band members, the music, and our followers were the center of my life. When I lost all that, I jumped with both feet into Buddhism, somewhat like someone who jumps into another relationship right after a divorce. This isn't to discount my love of Buddhism, which did eventually become more important than music for me. But clearly I hadn't processed that loss, and, as you'll learn, my Buddhist journey was not all about a sincere interest in the Dharma, but reflected some deeper pain and confusion that I was still working out—unconsciously.

A year after first hearing about Joseph Goldstein and the retreat in Joshua Tree, I was there myself. Two consecutive retreats were offered, so we signed up for both—a total of 22 days. We arrived late and had to sit in the front row, not my preference. The retreat was big, perhaps a hundred people or more. The teaching team was large, as well, and included Joseph, Jack Kornfield, and Anagarika Munindra, Joseph's Indian Buddhist teacher, as well as others. I was familiar with Jack from his book Living Buddhist Masters (now retitled Living Dharma). This was a remarkable set of interviews with legendary Theravada Buddhist teachers including Buddhist master Mahasi Sayadaw and Jack's own teacher Ajahn Chah.

Suffice it to say I was in awe of the people on the dais.

For perhaps ten days I felt like I was just repeating all the struggles of my previous retreats. The longed-for peace and insight always seemed just out of reach. But then everything changed. It would be many years before I would develop my own understanding of what happened that warm April afternoon in the High Desert.

It was just another sitting, my mind flitting here and there, no sense of stillness or real presence when, seemingly out of the blue I dropped into a feeling of calm, quiet, and peace. There were still thoughts, but they weren't bothering me. The shift actually felt more physical than mental. The tension and stress in the body dissolved. I felt grounded, rooted to the earth, at ease in a way I'd never felt in my life, at least never in my memory.

My immediate sense was that I had arrived, that this was what meditation was about, and I'd finally found it. I was wrong about that, but again, I only understand that in retrospect. What had happened was that I had experienced the first symptoms of samatha and samadhi, of tranquility and concentration. As pleasant and beneficial as those states are, they aren't the ultimate goals of practice. I will explore this topic more later, but let me just briefly say that in the Buddhist path, concentration is viewed as an essential foundation for the development of transformative insight. It has a key role. However, because the experience is so pleasant, even joyful at times, it's easy to believe you've reached the end or the goal of the path, and also easy to get attached—not to say addicted—to that pleasant experience. Many people who experience such peace wind up chasing the experience like any other addict. And so, it's vital to understand the role of concentration as well as its limits. Like all conditioned experiences it is impermanent, unsatisfactory, and not self. (Again, more on all this later.)

A few other moments stand out from that retreat.

Since my first retreat the previous Thanksgiving, I'd seen how people were invited to do service during the retreat, washing dishes, sweeping paths, cleaning bathrooms, and other tasks. When asked if I'd like to participate in this way, my first thought was, "I need to concentrate on meditating. Why would I waste my time doing dishes?" Talk about self-centered and misunderstanding the spirit of practice! One day during this retreat as I was dropping off my dishes after a meal, I was shocked to see that another teacher I had worked with in LA who was sitting the retreat as a student was washing the dishes. He smiled at me as I handed over my dirty plate. I walked away confused. Why would he lower himself to doing dishes? This is a moment in my memory that particularly highlights my spiritual (as well as emotional) immaturity. Even as I thought I was becoming so spiritual and "approaching" enlightenment, I clearly I had a long, long way to go. And I didn't have a clue.

Another moment from this retreat caused more confusion. Near the end of the three weeks I had a final interview with Jack Kornfield. My girlfriend and I had decided we were going to go on the three-month retreat that would be held at the Insight Meditation Society in the coming fall with many of these same teachers. This was an enormous commitment, especially considering what a relative newcomer I was to Buddhist meditation. I was driven by a sense that I had found the way to solve my life's pain, and one more long retreat would almost certainly complete the job. Again, my misunderstanding both of myself and of the practice was deep and broad. I had no idea where I was on the path, nor, in fact, how that path worked or what one could expect from it.

Sitting in the interview, outside under a blue desert sky I announced to Jack that I was coming to Massachusetts for the long retreat in the fall. I expected him to be impressed and perhaps to suggest that I would probably become enlightened while there. At least I expected praise. Instead, what he said was, "It's beautiful there in the fall." What? You're telling me about the weather? What about enlightenment? What about how brave I am to come?

I left the interview deflated, which was probably the point. Jack could easily see the grasping and delusion I was caught in. I'm sure it was clear to him the unreasonable expectations I had, and he wanted to bring me back down to earth.

Throughout this retreat I was working with the noting practice I described above. While I appreciated the structure of this practice which gave me something specific to do all the time, it did tend to become mechanistic and somewhat tedious. During those periods when I got into a more settled concentration, the noting subsided to a great extent, and I tended to simply focus on the breath and the pleasantly calm feeling.

On the last full day of the retreat, Joseph Goldstein introduced us to a practice that would wind up being very influential in the way I meditate to this day. He calls it "Big Mind." It takes us away from the ordinary way of understanding our human experience. While the noting practice is grounded in common perceptions--sensations, sounds, thoughts—Big Mind asks us to pay attention to something else, the mind itself, rather than its contents. This shift in perceptual orientation requires a somewhat steady state of mind, a good amount of concentration, which is presumably why Joseph held back this guidance until near the end of the retreat when we were all pretty settled from three weeks of silent practice. It draws from sources outside the Theravada and Vipassana traditions like Zen and Tibetan Buddhism.

Instead of giving instructions to do certain things like feel the breath or note thoughts, Big Mind is meant to help the mind enter a non-ordinary place and shift perception from that of a solid body and physical presence to more of a sense of an energetic field. It is "guidance," in the sense of leading our minds into this space—and, indeed, space plays a central role in the practice. The guidance has a poetic quality, asking us to imagine the mind like a vast sky; sensations like "stars in the night sky." He says, "No head, no shoulders, no back, chest, arms, legs, only points of sensation." Trying to break down our conception of solidness. He says, "Look directly at mind; clear, vast; without boundaries, limitless; it contains all things but isn't composed of them, "and "it is, but it doesn't exist." The guidance goes on like this, helping us to let go of our common perceptual framework and try on something different. Like Zen koan practice or Tibetan emptiness practices, we're trying to go beyond the limits that our conditioning place on our ability to experience the deepest realities. With enough concentration and guidance like this, some significant breakthroughs can happen.

After this period of meditation I was somewhat stunned. What just happened? Over the previous months I'd come to see the very structured forms of vipassana as the way you were "supposed" to meditate. I viewed noting and following the breath as challenges that I was supposed to perfect, and that some reward would come once I had achieved that. Now Joseph had just showed me a completely different way of meditating, one that didn't involve all the words and formal mental steps of vipassana, and yet took me to a place that felt more organic, expansive, and free.

After the retreat ended, I ordered a cassette recording of Joseph's "Big Mind" meditation. That summer, while I saved money by living at my parents' apartment in Pennsylvania while they were at their retirement home in Cape Cod, I often listened to his guidance. I loved where it took me.

Now my practice was taking shape. I could sit for longer periods without the knee pain overwhelming me. Although the deeper experiences of the three weeks in Joshua Tree gradually slipped away, I was still able, at times to get quite settled. I felt like a real meditator now, not just someone getting into the posture and faking it.

One weekend that summer I hitchhiked to Massachusetts for a weekend at the Insight Meditation Society (IMS) where the fall three-month retreat would be held. At the time an elder Burmese monk, Taungpulu Sayadaw, was leading a retreat and I got to sit in. A crusty old man who hadn't laid down to sleep in decades, this was the real thing. Skinny to the point of emaciation, his teaching was just as severe as his appearance. He emphasized the "32 parts of the body" meditation, from the famous Satipatthana Sutta. Here one was supposed to contemplate all the repulsive elements of the body: kidney, liver, spleen; bile, phlegm, feces; intestines, heart, lungs. I was alternately fascinated and disgusted. By now, though, I was all in with Buddhism and figured I should embrace the teachings no matter how far out they seemed.

On the personal level, that summer was pretty miserable. I wound up washing dishes in an Italian restaurant, but still couldn't save enough to pay for the retreat. I had to "borrow" money from my parents, who were not pleased about their 31-year-old son going off on some strange religious trip. At the same time, my girlfriend was drifting away from me. When I arrived at her home the day before the retreat, she essentially shut me out. I wound up getting drunk while watching TV with her mother, who didn't particularly like me and let me know why. I arrived at IMS with a brutal hangover, all set to sit a three-month silent retreat. Head aching, heart broken, ego crushed, I entered the silence bereft.

I should step out of this narrative now, because I've largely been ignoring the alcoholic/addict part of my story during these years. Certainly once I started meditation, and particularly during the time when I was immersed in Buddhist practice, my drinking and drugging decreased significantly. My use of drugs became intermittent, as did my drinking. But I still occasionally drank to excess, and I had no intention of quitting marijuana, as well as occasional hallucinogens. What's perhaps more salient to the whole story is that I was obviously trying to use meditation as another kind of fix or escape. And the way I dove in had all the earmarks of alcoholic extremes. Here, just a year after taking my first Buddhist meditation class, I was going into one of the most intense forms of practice: the three month "Rains Retreat." Looking back, it's clear that I was in over my head. The retreat itself would show that, and the aftermath even more. And, somehow, the fact that I arrived at this beautiful meditation center with a raging hangover captures everything you need to know about the imbalance and borderline insanity of it all.

Not much happens on a silent retreat. And yet, people invariably come out of it with stories to tell. Rarely, though, do these relate to meditation itself. Usually we just hear the funny or odd moments that happen outside the meditation hall. But I'm here to talk about meditation itself. And, again, there are some key moments that stand out in my recollection of that long-ago retreat.

First of all, despite my interest in "Big Mind" meditation, I began the retreat practicing noting again. This was probably because that's what was being taught. I didn't yet have a sense of ownership of my practice at that time. This is a critical turning point in any meditator's development, when you stop trying to follow the instructions given by some teacher and instead begin to follow your own instinct. During the first weeks of the retreat, I continued to struggle with noting, even though there was a good degree of settling. Two encounters with teachers began to shift my practice.

The first of these was with Joseph Goldstein, and it happened right after the morning meditation instruction. This was the period after breakfast when a teacher would give a guided meditation and then take questions. I wasn't one for raising my hand amid the hundred odd meditators, so after the sit I made my way up to the dais where Joseph was getting ready to walk off.

"Joseph," I whispered. "I'm settling in okay, but there's still this kind of dullness I'm feeling."

He turned to me and said, "Don't be afraid to feel."

Those five words, which I remember four decades later, began a major shift in my practice. Joseph had only encountered me once or twice and likely didn't even know my name. That means that my condition was probably a common one. At the time I was thrown back. Was I afraid to feel? What did that mean? I left the dais more confused than when I arrived.

I will say, since I am now a meditation teacher, it's a bit unnerving to realize that a somewhat offhand comment like that could stay with someone for essentially their whole life. It definitely gives me a sense of added responsibility in my own role.

In any case, I recall it as just a few days later that I was in an interview with Jack Kornfield when he told me something very similar: "Your practice is to feel."

The thing is, I thought of myself as a very emotional person, someone who felt a lot. But clearly these two teachers were seeing something different. So, I began a process of exploration. During walking meditation on the broad front lawn of the center on those beautiful fall days, I would ask myself, "What am I feeling?" If Joseph and Jack didn't think I was feeling what was going on, I had to figure out how to do that. How do you feel? Where are you supposed to place your attention to do that?

Jack gave me some hints about paying attention to my chest and belly, and I began to explore those areas. Eventually I concluded, rightly or wrongly, that the subtle sensations that appeared in that part of the body were the feelings they were talking about.

Now, you might wonder why I'm talking about feeling when my topic is meditation. That's because eventually paying attention to feeling—or in Buddhist terms "feeling tone"—became central to my practice and in fact my life. Trying to teach how to do that is also central to my approach.

It would take me many years before I would fully integrate this into my practice, but here the seeds were sown.

As you can imagine, it's impossible to sum up an entire three-month retreat in a few paragraphs or even pages. But let me share some of the ways my practice evolved over those months. As I said, I began the retreat using the noting practice again, and, as in the past, I'd often engage in a subtle or not-so-subtle struggle with that form. The mechanics of it tended to take over, blocking any more natural or organic

Sought Through Meditation

meditative experience, like Big Mind. It was quite a few weeks before this particular fever broke. (It's really hard to put timelines on a retreat like this without some kind of journal recording events.) My recollection is that one day I just gave up and dropped the noting.

Very quickly—again, memory here is tricky, but it seemed as if this happened in one sitting—I fell into an open space of awareness that felt natural, pleasant, and quite settled. It was a huge relief, and once again, I had the feeling I was figuring out how to meditate. The problem with that thought is that "how," isn't really the point of meditation. There are many helpful forms of meditation, but doing them "right," or "well," isn't why we practice. Rather the forms are meant to help the mind to arrive at a state from which there is clear seeing and the opportunity for insight to arise. Let me say that again: the forms are meant to help the mind to arrive at a state from which there is clear seeing and the opportunity for insight to arise.

In some ways or some sense, just hanging out in such a state can change how you experience or understand the world. Because such a state is based on letting go, the insight into suffering and the end of suffering can co-arise with the state.

Let me explain: when we meditate and see how our agitated mind is causing inner tension or stress, we are seeing how suffering is caused by clinging. We are taught to let go of thoughts when we notice them. If we keep doing that over and over (like on a retreat), we start to see how relief comes from letting go. Now we've experienced the first three Noble Truths: suffering, its cause, and its end. It is obvious, as well, that this is the result of following the Noble Eightfold Path—the Fourth Noble Truth: we are applying mindfulness and concentration with wise effort; living harmlessly (sila); with

Right View and Right Intention. And so, without any particularly special action, we develop insight into the Four Noble Truths just by practicing meditation (deeply). (See Appendix I for more on the Four Noble Truths and Noble Eightfold Path.)

Back to the retreat. It becomes difficult to describe practices like "open awareness," or "bare attention," in which there is little form, little structure. On a long retreat, what often happens is that the mind eventually just settles into a steady, calm state and many sittings just involve resting in that state. Little effort or inner direction is necessary. It's quite lovely.

As far as meditation goes, once I'd found this open space, I more or less rode out the retreat on that energy. And now here's the payoff: a three-month silent meditation retreat didn't fix me. That is the mistake we make when we try to make meditation our program (not that I even thought of it as a recovery program at that time). Meditation is the Eleventh Step, not the First Step. While I see it as a critical part of anyone's evolving recovery, it's not the starting point.

When the retreat ended I was a "good meditator," but my life was in shambles. I had nowhere to live, no job, no money, nothing. I went back to Boston, and over the next six months I gradually put a functioning life back together, as well as gradually falling back into drinking and using, sometimes to excess. I found a job in a spiritual bookstore, joined a band, and got an apartment. All good, right? Apparently not enough for me. Instead, I blew all that up again by falling for the siren call of a homeless New Age guru who promised more or less instant enlightenment. I left the job, the band, the apartment, and wandered off with him. A bizarre couple of months followed as we traveled the country as far as Hawaii and back. Eventually the demands of "living on faith" as he called it overwhelmed me. I drifted away, and by the end of summer, I was alone on a beach in Southern California wondering where I'd gone wrong. Now I was homeless, with no guru or anything else. It would take me another three years to build my life back up enough to even make it worth getting sober.

What had happened?

There are many ways to explain these tumultuous times in my life. We could say that I was "spiritually imbalanced." My meditation was way ahead of my emotional maturity. The intensity and depth of the three-month retreat caused a kind of psychic overload that I couldn't handle. Abandoning Buddhism and running off with a questionable teacher made as much sense as anything to me. I was adrift.

Becoming truly homeless—at one point I slept in a friend's VW bus for almost six months—woke me up. When you're just trying to find your next meal and a place to sleep, enlightenment slips down the list of priorities. A job and an apartment seem like heaven. After so many years of wanting to live an alternative lifestyle as a musician and then "spiritual seeker," now I just wanted an ordinary life. When I got sober, that's what my focus was. At the same time, when I saw the word "meditation" at that first meeting, I began to imagine a more integrated way of living, one that included a serious practice but didn't leave me disconnected from reality.

Now my meditation practice became part of a larger whole—Twelve Step work—and it acted as a support, not an end in itself. Even in those early years of sobriety I shared with friends about my practice and some of them followed me into the study of Buddhism. But it was at six years sober, solidly established in sobriety and on my way to a college degree and a brand-new life, that I finally felt safe enough to fully step back into Buddhist practice. And so began the journey that led me to *One Breath at a Time*, and the world of "Buddhist recovery."

Part II: Buddhist Meditation

The Background

Before I go further into this topic, it's important that you understand what I mean by "Buddhism." Like Christianity, the term Buddhism applies to a wide variety of sects and traditions. In brief, we can say there are three main branches: Theravada or the Southern Tradition, which is mainly practiced in Burma (Myanmar), Thailand, and Sri Lanka. This makes the claim as the oldest living tradition, taking the earliest extant literature (the Pali Canon) as its root source. Evolving later was the Mahayana, or Northern tradition. This encompasses Chinese Chan and Pure Land Buddhism, as well as Korean Soen and Japanese Zen. Later, the Tibetan or Varjaryana tradition arose in the Himalayan region. Each of these three traditions has a distinctive flavor and draws from different teachings. Up until the late twelfth century they intermingled in India, the Buddha's home, especially at the famous monastery at Nalanda. Here, apparently, monks of the three traditions studied and trained together, drawing from a vast library of literature compiled over more than a thousand years. Tragically, the monastery, and virtually all Buddhists in India were wiped out in a series of invasions from the West. The three traditions lost touch then, evolving in their own distinctive ways. It was only in the late nineteenth century that they once again became aware of each other. Today, we find all three traditions thriving in the West, where people have the opportunity to draw from a rich panoply of Buddhism.

However, those options can also cause confusion. Which tradition is best? What meditation is most effective? Who's got the goods? Such questions naturally arise when faced with these choices. I can only suggest that you sample the different traditions for yourself and see which one resonates for you.

My own choice was made long ago. I found myself drawn to the Western teachers who brought Vipassana meditation to the West in the 1970's. Joseph Goldstein, Jack Kornfield, Sharon Salzberg and others practiced in India, Burma, and Thailand and became very skilled at interpreting what they learned from the masters they encountered there, delivering the teachings in a palatable way for modern students. The fact that vipassana derived from the Theravada tradition wasn't even very clear at that time. Eventually, as I learned more, I was drawn more deeply into this ancient tradition.

The meditation practices I offer in this book come out of that tradition, although there's a certain blending with the other traditions that happens at times. My goal is certainly not to offer some pure version of a Buddhist tradition, but rather to help you navigate and cultivate a practice that will support your own goals.

With all these different traditions, not surprisingly Buddhist meditation can take many forms. The heart of all these forms, though, is mindfulness. What that word means and how to engage with it is a key element of this book. But mindfulness itself isn't the point. Yes, it has value in and of itself, but in the Buddhist scheme, mindfulness is a means to an end. And that end is insight, or in more lofty terms, awakening, enlightenment. We are trying to change both the way we see the world and how we experience it. The peace and equanimity that we develop in meditation changes how we experience the world. The insight that arises when we apply this special form of attention changes how we see the world. There are different ways to bring about these transformations, and the practice of mindfulness meditation is one of the most direct and efficient.

Practice

Meditation is a practice, meaning it's something we simply do. Like recovery, there's no end point, no graduation, no moving on to the next thing. It's how we live, and indeed, as we take our practice deeper, we try to embody the lessons of meditation in all the other aspects of our life as well.

Since I began meditating in 1978, I've always tried to do it "first thing" in the morning. Sometimes this meant right out of bed. Other times I'd have a cup of tea first or a shower. It all depended on the structure of my life at that point. Obviously you can meditate anytime you want or feel like it but I want to give you some reasons to do it first thing. For one, it requires stopping everything in your life, and that's really hard to do once your day is in full swing. For another, first thing means you haven't had time to build up a lot of stress or do a lot of thinking yet, so you are starting with the closest thing to a clean slate in your mind. Finally, meditation starts your day moving in the direction you want it to, toward calm, insight, and a sense of connection with yourself and the world. That's invaluable. It's a kind of statement of purpose to each day: this is who I want to be, how I want to live.

There are no tricks or magic to establishing a meditation practice. My one suggestion is that you schedule it into your day. Before going to bed at night, determine what time you will have to get up in order to fit in your meditation before work or other responsibilities start. Make a personal determination to prioritize this. You can do it.

As for the amount of time you practice, twenty minutes is considered to be a good base period. Less than that doesn't allow the mind to settle very much. Time is the irreplaceable element of meditation. There's a process that unfolds that depends upon it. Start with twenty minutes and then try to expand from that to thirty, forty-five, and possibly an hour.

You will soon discover that there is a qualitative difference between the shorter and longer times. To help you stick with the full period you commit to, it can be helpful to use a timer. (The Insight Timer app has pleasant bells rather than an alarm.)

If you are physically flexible enough, I recommend that you try to learn to sit on the floor cross-legged. The easiest way to do this is in the so-called "Burmese posture," in which the legs sit parallel on the ground. One typically uses the firm, round Japanese pillow called "zafu." A pad called a "zabuton" on which to perch your pillow is also helpful. Sitting on the floor in this way gives a particularly strong sense of groundedness, and the body will feel more stable than in a chair. If you aren't flexible enough for this posture, a meditation bench can be a good alternative. (I personally had to give up sitting on the floor some years ago when my knees gave out. I miss it.)

A chair is fine as well, just make sure you sit still. It's much easier to get fidgety in a chair than on the floor where everything is more or less locked in place.

Whatever your sitting situation, most important is sustaining the upright posture. Over time, as you become more attuned to your body in meditation, you will start to feel the difference between being aligned and not aligned. In alignment, the weight of the body rests on the buttocks. The head, shoulders, spine, and hips all line up. When we go out of alignment, the head will often tip forward pulling on the back muscles and causing strain.

In certain traditions, like Zen Buddhism, the posture is practically all that is taught in meditation. There can seem to be an almost military-like rigidity that is enforced. For myself, despite my best efforts (and what I am suggesting to you), I've rarely been able to hold my posture in this way. Whether this has had an actual negative impact on my meditation I don't know, other than the back pain that it has triggered.

In whatever way you are sitting, the emphasis should be on stillness. When we move the body, the mind tends to move as well. Nonetheless, perfection in this regard is also hard to attain, so that if we do need to move while sitting, we do so with great care, slowly and mindfully.

Meditation changes and evolves over time. It's important to understand that you aren't going to reach some level of perfection or that it will just steadily improve. Like your days, like your life, meditation goes up and down. You may feel you are making progress for a while, then it might seem as if you are falling back. Judging or scoring your meditation is not helpful. That only leads to more struggle and frustration. Acceptance is key. Mindfulness itself is just about seeing clearly what is happening right now, and that's all you can do with your meditation. That's not to say you can't make an effort or experiment with different techniques, but just don't get too caught up in the mechanics or trying to do it right. Trust that a process is playing out and that your job isn't to control that process but to show up on a consistent basis.

How to Meditate

Many of the practices described here are detailed in the "Guided Meditations" section of the book, as well as in audio recordings on my website, www.kevingriffin.net.

The Basics

There are lots of details to explore when learning meditation. However, it helps to keep it simple. When things start to feel complicated or overwhelming, return to these simple steps:

- Sit down.
- Start to follow the sensations of breath.
- When you realize the mind has wandered, gently bring it back to the breath.

The Details

Sit down: The way we hold our body is important in meditation. Upright, but not stiff; relaxed, but not slumping. If you can sit in a lotus posture, that's ideal. However, many people don't have the flexibility to do that. Sitting in a chair is fine. Sit on a firm but not hard chair. Avoid something like a soft couch because you will tend to sink in and slump.

Align the body so that the weight is held by the buttocks. When you find this point of balance it will feel as if the weight is channeled down the spine.

It's important to sit still. Moving the body is an act of restlessness, and it agitates the mind. This means, though, that you'll have to learn to sit with some discomfort at times. Working with pain in the body is another important piece of this process which I'll address later.

Follow the breath: This is the most common form of meditation. We are using the breath as what's called an "anchor."

Other things can be the anchor: a mantra; a visualization; other sensations in the body; sound. Anything that you can place the attention on can be an anchor. The breath is useful because it's always there and it's not particularly pleasant or unpleasant. It's just a natural and neutral sensation.

The standard instructions say you can follow the breath at the nostrils or the belly. At the nostrils you are feelings the sensation of air touching as it flows in and out. At the belly you are aware of the sensations of movement, up and down. The point is to find something you can feel and stick with it. These sensations can vary greatly in intensity. The breath often becomes more subtle as the mind gets quieter. That means you have to pay closer attention, which has the benefit of strengthening the concentration.

Other ways to work with the breath include making a soft mental note, "In, out," if you're following the breath at the nostrils, or "Rising, falling," if you're following the breath at the belly. The words are just meant to help you sustain the attention. Don't let the words distract you from the actual sensations.

When the mind wanders: dealing with distracting thoughts, emotions, and sensations is perhaps the most challenging and important aspect of becoming a meditator. Often people make their meditation a kind of competition and see thoughts as a sign of their failure. This is the wrong attitude. Thoughts are natural. We can't just turn them off. However, with regular practice you will learn to work with thoughts so that they will not only stop being a problem, but will actually be a source of insight, spiritual and personal growth.

To begin practice, we just want to develop the habit of letting go of thoughts and returning to the breath, without inner commentary. So, whenever you notice the mind has

wandered from the breath, just bring the attention back to the sensations of breathing. This can happen many times during a period of meditation. You might be lost for a long time before realizing you are thinking. None of this matters. Just stick with the process. Trust the process. Keep it simple.
Noting: One tool that can help you to stay focused is the practice called "noting" that I mentioned earlier. This can be as simple as saying (silently) "In, out," to track the inhalations and exhalations. It can also be expanded to note "thinking, thinking," "hearing, hearing," "feeling, feeling," when you experience one of these. Repeating the word helps to interrupt the thoughts.

This can then be further refined to note types of thoughts: "desire, desire," "planning, planning," "remembering, remembering," etc. This practice has two effects: it interrupts the wandering or distracted mind, plus it reveals some of the habit patterns of thinking. In that way, we start to learn about our own conditioning.

Noting should be used lightly. If it starts to become obsessive, or you are straining to name or identify things, back off. This isn't about perfectly tracking every movement of mind. It's just meant to help you gain clarity and calm.
Counting Breaths: You can also count the breaths in various ways. One common approach is to note "in" on the in-breath and on the out-breath count, like this: "In, one; in, two; in, three," up to ten. You then return to one. If you lose count, go back to one and start again. This is a repetitive practice, but it can be helpful when the mind is very busy and you're having a hard time just establishing some concentration.
Gathas: Another way to work with the breath comes from Thich Nhat Hanh, the late Vietnamese Zen Master. He suggests repeating these words with the breath:

> In, out
> Deep, slow
> Calm, ease
> Smile, release,
> Present moment, wonderful moment

As with counting, the primary focus remains on the sensations of breath. The words simply act as guard rails to keep you from getting lost.

How It Works

It can be helpful to understand the elements of meditation we are talking about. Although it's not necessary to have this information, it can help you identify what needs development in your practice.

In Buddhist meditation there are three key elements: effort, mindfulness, and concentration. Effort is the engagement and persistence applied to practice. Mindfulness is present moment awareness imbued with a certain wisdom and understanding. Concentration is the calming and focusing aspect that allows you to sustain mindfulness, and thus look more deeply at your experience.

Everything starts with effort. Not striving or struggling, but showing up and placing the attention on our breath or other anchor. There isn't just one level of effort we apply or one technique. Rather, we monitor our progress, the changing qualities of agitation or calming, of clarity or confusion, of sleepiness or energy, and then respond to those qualities with appropriate forms and levels of effort. If we are having a hard time focusing, we apply more energy; if we have settled in, we can back off and let the practice flow. Skillfully applying effort implies, then, knowledge of various techniques of practice. At times we'll sense the need for a calming practice or one that softens the heart. We might need to bring in self-compassion or focus on underlying emotions. Becoming a meditator means developing a working knowledge of a variety of approaches and responses. It takes time to build these skills, and that too is part of effort, sustaining our practice for the long haul. Ultimately, skillful effort depends upon applied mindfulness to uncover the wise response to any moment's mind/body experience.

Mindfulness has the role of guiding you to see and understand what is happening in your mind and body. It is meant to function as an unbiased interpreter of experience, a reality check, so to speak. While, for instance, we might feel some pain in our back that we resist and want to change, mindfulness asks us to simply feel the sensations on the raw, visceral level, as well as noticing the resistance and wish to change. And so, instead of automatically moving the body or getting up to stretch and make the pain go away, we learn to sit with it and learn what it has to teach us. It turns out that pain and resistance contain deep wisdom when we are able to view them with curiosity and interest. Here we begin to see the impermanent nature of things and the ways we create suffering. Mindfulness, then, is not just a recorder of events, but implies an investigation into the underlying causes and processes by which our mind/body states arise and cease. What are we seeking? What is driving us? What illusions do we hold? How can we let go? All these questions and more inform our mindfulness practice.

In order to get to this level of attention, though, we must sustain the mindfulness, and that's where concentration comes in. Concentration requires persistence and patience, the willingness to stick with what can be a tedious process. It requires time and the ability to tolerate the agitation that blocks its arising. Concentration allows us to let go of tension and resistance, to breathe, relax, and move the attention into a difficult experience, instead of trying to move away. The payoff is a tranquil mind and body, serene and peaceful, a deep feeling of satisfaction and even bliss.

In practical terms, concentration develops by persistently returning to the "object" of meditation, the breath, mantra, or other focus. Each time we become aware of the wandering mind or other distraction, we bring the attention back. This involves letting go of the thought, which is at the heart of the process. We begin to see how attached we are to thinking, how habitual and compulsive it is. At first, simply drawing the attention back to the breath might not seem to be doing much. It takes real patience and a willingness to sit with all the agitation that arises to establish concentration. Until that happens, you have to trust in the process.

More on Mindfulness

In traditional Buddhist teachings, there are four areas where we can apply mindfulness, called the "Four Foundations of Mindfulness." These are body, feelings, mind, and phenomena. To understand what these terms specifically refer to and how to apply our mindfulness in these areas, we need to go through them carefully.

"Body" first refers to being aware of all the sense experiences we have: seeing, hearing, tasting, touching, and smelling. This, then, includes mindfulness of the breath which is actually the awareness of touch, the touch of air and movement of the body. The Buddha also talks about being aware of posture, first in terms of sitting erect, and then whether we are sitting, standing, walking, or lying down. Further we're encouraged to be aware of the impermanence of the body, its components, and the elements that make it up. Finally, we're taught to be aware of every activity of the body, like reaching out an arm or bending over, eating, drinking, urinating, and so forth. When encountering this teaching, we begin to see that what at first seems simple and obvious, is actually quite expansive and demanding. To maintain mindfulness of all these bodily activities is a challenge that only the most devoted students—and often only monastics—can manage. That's okay. Perfection, while a fine goal, is not a helpful measure of the success of our practice. Simply sustaining our effort is more important than achieving particular results. It's also clear that this teaching applies to more than meditation itself. Mindfulness is a practice for the whole of our lives.

Mindfulness of the body is the easiest reference point to bring us back to the present moment. Whether in meditation or in ordinary daily activities, remembering to just feel the breath or the feet or any other part of the body—any sensation—quickly wakes us up. If you want to develop a meaningful mindfulness practice, this is the place to start—and the place to return to over and over.

Mindfulness of feeling has a specific meaning in Buddhist teachings, although I think it's helpful to expand on that meaning. Specifically, it refers to the pleasant, unpleasant, or neutral quality of any physical or mental experience. So, you smell baking bread, and it's pleasant. You stub your toe, and it's unpleasant. You walk down the street, and it's neutral. You think about your upcoming vacation, and it's pleasant. You remember a mistake you made at work, and it's unpleasant. You make your grocery list, and it's neutral. The importance of applying mindfulness to these experiences is that the pleasant ones tend to lead to desire or grasping. The unpleasant ones tend to lead to aversion. The neutral ones tend to lead to inattention. All three of these tendencies lead to dukkha, suffering or unsatisfactoriness. If we can bring mindfulness to these tendencies and let them go, we, by definition, can end dukkha. The first benefit of noticing feeling on this level is that it helps us to take things less personally or make a story out of experiences. We simply realize, "That was unpleasant," and move on. It simplifies things.

In my experience, it's helpful—vital even—to stretch this traditional idea of feeling to include emotions and moods. Bringing mindfulness and care to these experiences is the beginning of moving through them, of managing our relationship to emotional states. I explore the approach to doing this below in "Changing Our Relationship to Difficult Emotions."

Mindfulness of mind also has a specific meaning or meanings in Buddhist thought. It refers to states of mind like lust, anger, and confusion; concentration, distraction, and agitation. I find this a bit abstract and subjective. Many of these mind states seem fluid and hard to pin down. Nonetheless, as with feeling, observing mind states can help us to detach from them. In fact, here we may begin to notice the interaction of mind, feelings, and body. While this practice guides us to divide them into categories, in lived experience, they are interconnected. Sensations trigger feelings and feelings trigger mind states and thoughts. Thoughts trigger feelings and feelings trigger sensations. They're all working together in the mind/body system.

Most meditators will look on this foundation as being about observing thoughts. This is the most common challenge in practice, the tendency to get lost in thoughts. How we work with thoughts is key to our practice. I'll explore this further below in "Working with Thoughts."

The fourth foundation is where we apply our understanding of the Dharma to our experience. Here, again, we are encouraged to let go of the personal view and see the elements of mind and body as impersonal, a natural process unfolding. I think of this as "The Big Picture." What's really going on? If we don't take our experiences personally, what do we see? We are guided here to remember the Three Characteristics of Existence: impermanence, unsatisfactoriness (suffering), and not-self. Everything is unstable and in the process of change; because of this, we can never arrive at permanent satisfaction; if everything is constantly changing, where is the solid self experiencing all of it? What we see is a continuous process of change with no center, no core. When we deeply understand this viewpoint, we cease to be caught up in the dramas of life, the ever-changing ups and down. Now we find the peace of equanimity.

Mindfulness with Breathing

While using the breath as the focus of meditation is a common practice, there is a particular teaching, or sutta, devoted to mindful breathing that gives more specific instruction. Called the "Anapanasati Sutta," or the Discourse on Mindfulness of Breathing, this teaching follows the Four Foundations of Mindfulness. There are sixteen steps to this process. These steps can be used as guidelines to moving deeply into meditation. They also function as something of a map of the meditative experience itself. In this way they point to natural stages in the evolution of a mindfulness practice. (You will find instructions on this practice in the "Guided Meditations" section below.)

Please note that, while my description here is just a few paragraphs, the process itself unfolds slowly. Many people spend an entire meditation retreat of multiple days or even weeks, working through these steps. You can do them all in one sitting, but until you gain familiarity with them, it's best

Sought Through Meditation

to take your time on each one.

This practice starts, of course, with establishing attention on the breath. You can do this in whatever way you like. You might pay attention to the sensations at the nostrils or the movement of the belly. You might follow the whole breath through the body. You can count the breaths or note the breath. Anything that stabilizes the attention on the breath itself.

From there you expand the attention to include the whole body, while maintaining a certain amount of attention on the breath. This is the key characteristic of this practice, that you are always paying attention to the breath along with something else. That "something else" evolves as you move through the steps.

Continue to feel the breath and the whole body until the body becomes calm.

Now you move to the second foundation of mindfulness, feeling. Here you look for any pleasant feelings that are arising out of the calmness of the body. Continuing to feel the breath with those pleasant feelings.

The next instruction is to "experience the mental formation." This means we bring an increasingly subtle awareness to how thoughts form. The impulses, the triggers, the feelings, and underlying tendencies of our mind. Breathe with feelings as you watch thoughts arise. Stay with this experience until the thoughts start to settle as well.

This leads us to the third foundation, awareness of the mind with the breath. Begin here by observing what your mind state is: grasping or letting go; harmonious or disturbed; calm or agitated. If your attention gets especially refined, you may notice that sensations and feelings are all experienced through the mind or in the mind. See that there is more to the mind than the elements of experience. We call this "the space of mind," or "awareness itself." Breathing and sensing this, notice the pleasant mental experience of simply being with awareness. Let concentration coalesce around the space of mind and breath. See that the hindrances and difficulties in meditation have now fallen away.

The final stage, the big picture, starts with seeing the impermanent nature of experience as you breathe. This leads to realizing how unsatisfactory all experience is—it keeps changing, so it can't offer final release. This changing nature also reveals that there is no stable core or self experiencing all this. Everything is flow, sensations, feelings, and mind states.

There's nothing to do with this realization but let go. Let go of attachments to body, to feelings, to thoughts, and to the sense of self.

This is Anapanasati. It takes us through all the elements of experience and exposes the underlying reality. We can use this framework to guide our meditation. We can also use it to identify what is happening in our meditation. While we don't need to force our meditation to follow these exact steps, they can be useful as pointers. Meditation can take us to deep, quiet places that don't have labels on them. This sutta can help us to understand where we are in the meditative process and what is happening.

More on Concentration

When most people hear the word "meditation," the quality they think of is concentration. They imagine a serene, empty mind, perhaps one infused with bliss. This kind of state isn't the goal of mindfulness meditation, though it can arise with lots of practice. For the busy-minded, easily distracted Western student of meditation, concentration is probably the most difficult quality to develop. It requires patience, persistence, and determination. Some people have a particular talent for concentration, while most of us must work hard for it.

What is the importance of concentration in mindfulness practice?

Mindfulness brings us more fully into the present moment. Concentration lets us more fully penetrate that moment. While a moment of mindfulness helps us to see clearly what is arising, sustained, concentrated mindfulness allows us to see more deeply. The reality we are experiencing becomes more vivid and stands out in starker relief.

The pleasure we experience with concentration can actually distract us from its more vital purpose, cultivating insight. As the mind becomes more still, the Three Characteristics of Existence, impermanence, unsatisfactoriness, and not-self, become clearer. Less caught in our personal drama, these truths come to the forefront of our consciousness. While we can see these realities in ordinary mindfulness meditation, concentration makes them clearer, more obvious. That vision is what leads to transformative insight.

Time is perhaps the most important factor in developing concentration. Whether on a multi-day retreat or simply a longer morning meditation period, time helps the mind and body settle. There's no tool that creates instant concentration. Nonetheless, there are practices that can help.

First is what's called "aim and sustain." This means that we take particular care in bringing attention to the object of concentration, typically the breath. In this way, rather than just being aware that we are breathing, we try to feel the specific details of the sensations and follow the whole breath from start to finish. That is the "aiming." Then we try to connect to the next breath with continuous awareness, "sustaining." When we can get this kind of attention going for a few minutes, a qualitative shift in concentration can develop.

Another way of working on concentration is to use a

repetitive or structured meditation object. Counting breaths and using mantras are two common repetitive practices. With counting we typically go one-to-ten breaths then start again at one. If we lose count, we simply go back to one. Mantras are even more simple, usually a sacred word we repeat over and over in the mind. Both practices have the tendency to quiet the mind by letting it settle into a simple, repeating pattern.

An example of a structured practice is loving kindness meditation. Here we use phrases, images, and the breath to move through a series of categories of people to whom we send loving thoughts. This kind of meditation gives the mind a lot to do, thus helping to keep it on track.

(Guided instructions for all these practices are found later in the book.)

Two other factors that influence concentration are posture and stillness. Upright posture on a stable surface is important. Slumping into a soft couch tends to make for a dull mind, which is not conducive to the clarity needed for concentration.

Stillness of body supports stillness of mind. When we are able to hold the body with no movement it has the effect of bringing any movements of mind into relief, thus allowing us to quickly come back to the object.

Technically, concentration practice is distinct from mindfulness meditation. Nonetheless, it's apparent that in order to sustain concentration, you need to know if the mind is on the object or not. That means you have to be mindful of where the attention is. Mindfulness has a broader purpose than concentration alone, but it is also a part of such a practice.

Concentration is powerful. It can create remarkable altered states and levels of inner peace. The Buddha praised it as a wholesome form of "non-sensual pleasure." Even more important, concentration brings clarity to the mind, allowing us to see deeply into reality, into the Dharma, with profound benefits.

Challenges to Practice

The mechanics of meditation aren't particularly complicated or, strictly speaking, difficult. What makes meditation challenging is that we can't control our minds and bodies to the degree that we'd like to. Our minds wander; our bodies become uncomfortable; our emotions bubble up. Those are realities. The challenge of meditation is to respond to those realities skillfully.

This brings us to what's called "Right Effort." Our effort in meditation must be careful, gentle, and persistent. When the mind wanders it's easy to fall into the trap of getting frustrated or judging yourself, thinking you are failing. But meditation isn't a competition; there is no winning or losing. The only losing is when we don't do it or when we quit. Rather we can think in terms of creating suffering or ending suffering; becoming more comfortable or less comfortable.

Right Effort is traditionally defined in four ways:

1. The effort to avoid unwholesome states (or behaviors) that aren't happening right now.

2. The effort to let go of unwholesome states (or behaviors) that have us in their grip.

3. The effort to create wholesome states that aren't happening right now—called "cultivating."

4. The effort to sustain wholesome states that are here right now

While this is a somewhat mechanistic way of looking at experience, there are some recovery parallels that might illuminate our understanding.

"Avoiding" is what we do when we don't go to the bar or

the dealer's house anymore; when we "don't drink or use no matter what." It's how we stay out of trouble.

Letting go is perhaps the most important action we take in recovery. Letting go of our addiction, letting go of anger and resentment, and letting go of old ideas. Letting go is also the essence of meditation, as we let go of thoughts and come back to the breath.

Creating wholesome states is what much of our recovery work is trying to do. Going to meetings, working the Steps, talking to newcomers. When we "suit up and show up," we are going against our negative impulses in order to create new, more healthy and productive habits. In meditation, we are also trying to create new mental habits, new "neural pathways," the connections in the brain that become our default tendencies.

Sustaining these positive states is the daily work of recovery. One day at a time, we do the next right thing. When we meditate, we use concentration to sustain positive states.

Another way to look at effort in meditation is to see it as balancing energies. Not too tight, not too loose. If our effort is tense or anxious, striving or forced, we create more suffering. If we just sit there spacing out, we fall into lethargy. An important aspect of meditation practice is to track the quality of effort and keep inclining toward balance. This can only be learned through practice.

The Five Hindrances

The experience of meditation can often seem chaotic and confusing. We sit down and before we know it we're swept away with different thoughts and feelings, different energies and emotions. The Buddha helps us understand all these forces by categorizing them as Five Hindrances. When we look at our meditative experience, we'll often find that these are playing a big part. Dividing up our difficulties into these categories helps us make sense of their nature and clarifies what is happening. With this growing clarity, we feel less overwhelmed, and the mind can start to settle.

Here are the five hindrances:

- Desire

- Aversion

- Sloth and torpor (sleepiness)

- Restlessness and worry

- Doubt

Identifying these as they arise in our meditation is a valuable step forward in practice. As we get more familiar with these common challenges, they become less bothersome and more like traffic jams or lines at the grocery store: minor annoyances that we don't take personally.

Desire: Desire heads the list because it's so common, so persistent, and is identified by the Buddha as the "cause of suffering." Our habitual efforts to control things, to acquire things, to feel and understand things undermine our serenity. This tendency keeps us on a treadmill—called "samsara"—that acts as a feedback loop. The more we feed our desire, the more persistent it becomes. As addicts, we recognize that desire was at the root of our problems. When we start to meditate and watch the mind, we begin to see where and how that problem originated.

In meditation, the first thing we want to do with desire is identify it, which is true of all five hindrances. Once we see it, we have the potential to let it go. As long as it's obscured it works behind the scenes and we have no control over it.

Once we've identified desire, usually by simply noticing that we are thinking about something we want, we next want to learn to feel it. What does desire feel like in the body? What's the emotional tone or mood that goes with it? Quickly we will realize that it doesn't feel good, in the body or in the mind. This, then, gives us the motivation to let it go. We aren't letting go of desire because it's "bad," but because it doesn't make us happy. It's fundamentally unpleasant and unsatisfying.

Desire can take many forms: craving sense pleasure (food, sex, beauty), grasping after feelings (happiness, calm), desire for intimacy, or wanting material things. Desire can also be mental, wanting to know something, to figure something out, to understand something. As you develop your meditation practice, start to become familiar with the many forms of desire.

Instruction: As you are meditating, when you notice your mind has wandered, notice if the thought was one of desire, feel it in the body, feel it in the mind. Return the attention to the breath.

It is important to point out that the desire the Buddha refers to as the cause of suffering is a certain type of desire, an unwholesome one. It's also true that there is wholesome desire, the desire for spiritual growth, or to be helpful, kind, and generous. Ultimately the Buddhist path is about cultivating this wholesome desire while letting go of the unwholesome.

Aversion: Aversion is the flip side of desire: the wish not to feel somthing, to not have something. Aversion also takes many forms: fear, anger, resentment, distaste. Like desire, it can be sense based—having pain in the body or smelling an unpleasant odor. We can have aversion to people, to experiences, to work or responsibilities. In its most pernicious form, aversion turns back on ourselves, on our emotions, our thoughts, or simply not liking ourselves. Like desire, it originates in the mind.

Aversion takes the form of judgment. We take a stance against someone, something, or some idea. We build a belief system around our own viewpoint. In this way, aversion becomes solidified in the mind. It's important that we reflect on these habits and begin to see that judgments are just conditioned thoughts, not true or false, just ideas that we attach to. *Instruction:* As you are meditating, when you notice your mind has wandered, notice if the thought was one of aversion, feel it in the body, feel it in the mind. Return the attention to the breath.

Sloth and Torpor: The third hindrance turns the focus from the mind to the body, from thoughts and emotions to energetic states. In practical terms sleepiness arises in meditation because we get too relaxed without the needed balance of vigor. In some ways, then it's a good sign, a sign that the meditation is working. There are some antidotes, but first it's important to just bring mindfulness to the experience, to become aware when sleepiness is arising and see what it feels like.

To change this tendency, see if it would be helpful to meditate at a different time of day. For many people morning is the best time to sit. Experiment and see what's best for you. As soon as you notice sleepiness coming, open your eyes. Letting in light is one of the best antidotes. Make sure your posture is erect, not slumping. Don't sit on too soft a cushion, like a feather bed or couch that you sink into.

Sleepiness can also be emotional. Depressive states make the mind dull. If this is the case, it's better to exercise before meditating so as to raise the energy and mood. Be careful that sloth and torpor doesn't turn into negative rumination. Watch the thought patterns that emerge from this state and let them go.

To counter this energy in meditation, open the eyes, straighten the posture, and take a few deeper breaths. Like everything else, sloth and torpor is impermanent. Try to sit through it.

Restlessness and Worry: The flip of sloth and torpor, this hindrance sets you squirming on your meditation seat. The urge to move can get overwhelming. The traditional antidote is a repetitive concentration practice, like counting the breaths. If the state feels claustrophobic, focus on the spacious quality of the mind. Listen to sounds that take you out of that enclosed feeling.

Like sleepiness, restlessness often has an emotional component, in this case, anxiety. This must be approached with care. These feelings usually carry a story along with them that complicates the process. Much of our meditative work ends up being about dealing with such feelings and stories. Learning to hold what comes at us is the art of practice. I will talk further about this later.

To deal with restlessness as you sit, try intentionally relaxing the body, one part at a time. Take some deeper, calming breaths and feel the restlessness as energy rather than a problem that has to be solved. Let it come and let it go.

Doubt: Doubt can take many forms. Before we get into recovery we might doubt we are addicts. When first engaging the Twelve Steps we might doubt they would work. Or we have doubts about God. Or doubts about meditation helping us. Doubts about Buddhism. It's important that we look into our biases and judgments when we see any of these forms of doubt arising. They can be huge impediments on our path of recovery.

In meditation, doubt often arises about our practice. People get the idea that they aren't good at it or that they have some personal failing that makes them uniquely incapable of practicing. Sitting down and bringing awareness to your body and mind is difficult. Simply reining in the stream of thoughts can feel overwhelming. If we take what happens personally, when faced with the previous four hindrances it's easy to get the idea that we can't do it. However, as with recovery itself, the only way to fail is to quit. If you can keep showing up on your cushion or chair, you will work through all of these challenges and more.

And so, the most important thing about doubt is to keep a perspective. When we see what is happening as natural, not personal; as organic to the process, not unique to us, then we can ride out the ups and downs much more easily. Doubt itself is a natural element of this.

In the same way doubt often comes up around the Buddhist teachings. We can get confused by terms like "emptiness" or "no self." What's most useful is to continue to practice and continue to study. As your meditation deepens and your understanding of the Dharma expands, many doubts will dissipate. "More will be revealed," as the Big Book says.

Working with Thoughts

For most people, the first, and often the continuing challenge of meditation is how we respond to the busyness of our minds, the flood of thoughts that we encounter when we sit down and try to focus our attention. It's a common misconception that meditation requires stopping thinking. This is not the case.

The first task with thoughts is to realize they are there.

Normally we don't know that we are thinking, and in meditation this habit continues. When we sit down and put the attention on the breath it will typically wander off pretty quickly. We need to be alert to this. Once we realize that we're thinking instead of paying attention to the breath, we can simply come back and start again. This moment of noticing thoughts is a critical one.

At this point people will often start to judge themselves or get frustrated by the wandering mind. This only compounds the problem. The fact that you got lost in thinking isn't a failing on your part. If we allow ourselves to get frustrated, we will just become more agitated and stir up another round of thoughts. Instead, we need to develop an attitude of patience and acceptance. Thoughts are natural; we're not trying to achieve some special state. Mindfulness is about seeing what is happening, not controlling what is happening.

Once we are able to develop this attitude of acceptance, we can apply other strategies to thoughts. First of these is to notice what type of thought we are having, or what its theme is. In this way we start to see what mental patterns we have, thus learning more about our own mind. Perhaps you worry a lot about money or like to drift off in fantasies. Maybe you have a lot of resentments or regrets. When we can see these patterns, we can respond to and change them. The first response we can bring is to remember that right now we are just sitting here breathing. Whatever thoughts arise are about the past or future. They don't have to be addressed right now. We can let them go.

These insights also become applicable to our daily lives. We'll see that what happens in meditation happens outside meditation as well. We'll see how our behavior, moods, and perceptions are all colored by these patterns of thought. If

Sought Through Meditation

we bring mindfulness to them in our daily lives we become less under their sway. Instead of reacting right away or falling into a distressing mood, we can step away, realize that we're lost in thoughts, and settle down. There may be some lingering emotional aftereffects of troubling thoughts, but with mindfulness, we learn to breathe with those feelings, accept them, and trust that they will pass if we don't keep feeding them with more unhelpful thoughts.

Finally, watching thoughts is another way to detach from "selfing." We see that, as one teacher says, "Your mind has a mind of its own." They don't belong to you. You don't control them. They keep changing. They really aren't personal. They're just conditioned mental habits that, when seen clearly, can be abandoned. This is the way to true freedom.

One traditional response to unhelpful or unwholesome thoughts is called "replacing." Here we intentionally bring in a more helpful or supportive thought to counter the one that is showing up. A good example of this is using loving kindness to counter anger. (More on this in the "Heart Practices" section.) I especially like to reflect on self-compassion when I am struggling with negative self-talk. Here I simply remind myself of something like, "This situation is difficult," or "I'm okay." A simple "snap out of it" thought can interrupt such harmful ideas, what one teacher calls "the Inner Tyrant." This goes to an important element of our practice: not using mindfulness as a sledgehammer with which to pound ourselves. Many people fall into this trap. They have the idea of meditation as a kind of self-improvement program, and when their thoughts reveal some perceived deficiency in their personality or in their life, they start berating themselves. The irony is that someone who sets out to learn meditation is probably already a pretty good person. Certainly not someone who deserves abuse.

So, here is another place we can use the "Big Picture" view. Remembering that you are doing this to bring more peace and care into your life helps you to let go of the perfectionism that leads to self-tyranny.

Changing Our Relationship to Difficult Emotions

The idea that meditating might bring up difficult feelings doesn't usually occur to us when we begin to practice. More likely we're focused on developing calm or joy or even some altered states. However, meditation is not an escape from our lives or ourselves. In fact, it is more like an intensification of our ordinary experience. In that way, we may find quite strong emotions arising as we meditate. Barring that, more subtle, unacknowledged or unnoticed feelings can undermine our practice. We might get lost in thoughts over and over, not realizing that there is some hidden, underlying emotion triggering those thoughts. Here we need to take a different tack in our practice.

The goal in this process is to begin to feel emotions merely as energetic states, to disengage from them as having meaning or being threatening or dangerous. There is often a story we tell ourselves about our feelings, and this tends to feed rather than weaken the emotion. These thoughts also block us from directly experiencing feelings. We can spend a lot of time talking about and thinking about our emotions without ever having direct contact with them. To "feel feelings" can seem like a mysterious task as we move into a non-verbal, non-material realm.

Before we can even begin this process we have to deal with the underlying fear we have about feeling our emotions. Many of our typical strategies for handling emotions are ways to get away from or think our way out of our feelings because we don't want to actually be with them.

Since the essence of this practice is to be present for our lives, we need to start by feeling that fear.

Here we are feeling ourselves breathing, and then we are trying to sense what fear feels like. If we can get close to it, we'll see that it's highly energetic. It is sending energy throughout the body. While it can help to locate specific sensations, maybe in the face, or hands, or belly, or anywhere else, I like to just have a sense of my whole body. Try to just feel your whole body and let the fear or the energy move through as you breathe.

Once you're able to let go of the fear—the resistance to feeling—you can move on to actually being with any anxiety, sadness, anger, or other emotion underneath. This involves doing essentially the same thing you did with the fear. Breathing, giving the feeling "space" in the body and mind to just be there. Being aware of the energetic quality. These feelings often show up strongly in the chest or belly, so let that area be a focus. Notice the tendency to slip into thinking or fixing or figuring out the feeling, and return to the felt experience with the breath.

Essentially this is the practice. You're trying to stay tuned to this visceral level, just feelings, just energy, not fall into thoughts and stories about what the feelings mean or what you should do about them. Just feel.

You'll notice that the feeling is dynamic, not static. It has different nuances and keeps changing, however subtly. See if you can just allow this to happen without doing anything about it, either running away, shutting down, distracting yourself, or creating a story.

Doing this will not automatically make the feelings go

away. The anxiety, sadness, or anger might hang around. What we're trying to do is not so much stop feeling a particular way, but stop seeing it as such a problem. Just allow these energies to be there.

One critical component of this process is to remember that these feelings will not last. They are impermanent. It often can feel as if they are stuck in us or that if we don't get rid of them we'll be overwhelmed. This is just a thought. So, the last element of this practice is to notice when you aren't feeling the feeling. This then reassures you that the feelings will come and go, so you don't have to be afraid of them. They are just energies. They don't have any intrinsic meaning. They are part of being human. Normal. There's nothing wrong with feeling them.

Working with Physical Pain

Our bodies aren't designed to sit still for long periods of time. That means that as we extend our meditation sessions or go on retreat, discomfort will almost certainly arise. It might be pain in the knees from sitting cross-legged. It might be pain in the back. Unpleasant sensations can appear anywhere in the body. Working with them is a critical piece of the process.

The natural response to pain is aversion, not liking it and wanting it to go away. And because aversion is one of the hindrances to meditation, we are challenged to let it go. This is the first task of working with discomfort. As soon as we notice pain, rather than trying to change our posture or fix it in some way, we check in with aversion. This takes courage and patience. Not reacting to pain is counter to all our instincts.

The breath is a valuable partner here. Connect with the breath as you feel the tension and resistance arising. Breathe into the unpleasant sensation, relax the body, and release the tension. Now, instead of being overwhelmed by the restless urge to move, you experience the pain in a larger space. Without the hindrance of aversion blocking your awareness, you can begin to examine the sensation itself. Here we apply classic mindfulness teachings, noticing the qualities of the sensation: heat, pressure, tingling, heaviness, lightness, flow, and stasis. By changing our perception of the experience from "pain," to "sensation," we neutralize the mental reaction. Awareness and curiosity lead the mind rather than craving and aversion.

Just as with difficult emotions, a useful element of this exploration is watching the impermanent nature of the sensation. While ordinary consciousness perceives pain as solid, when mindfulness is applied, we see that such sensations are constantly moving, shifting, growing, and shrinking. As we breathe with all this, the sense of pain as a problem changes. Neither good nor bad, it is simply sensation.

In practice, such an attitude is difficult to sustain for long periods. What typically happens is that the mindfulness and concentration slip and the body quickly tenses, triggering aversion. We can use that moment as a mindfulness bell, a reminder to reapply our attention with equanimity. If we stick with this process, returning over and over to a non-reactive awareness of unpleasant sensation, it can foster strong concentration states.

What I've just described is an ideal, and we need to be careful about getting overly invested in ideals. At times pain in meditation will become unmanageable. It doesn't help to push yourself or to grit your teeth and try to get through it. That's not the point at all. We need to take care of ourselves. Each of us will have a different capacity for this work and tolerance for this challenge. Be kind to yourself. When working with pain becomes unmanageable or overwhelming, let up. Change posture or stop sitting all together. There is no special benefit to forcing yourself to meditate through pain.

Meditation and the Twelve Steps

For many years I worked with the Twelve Steps in the traditional manner, and I found that immensely helpful in my personal growth and healing. There was a lot of work I needed to do. Arriving at my first meeting as an unemployed musician, high school dropout, and serial failure at relationships meant meditation wasn't the most important part of my program for those early days of sobriety. Eventually, though I went back to school, started working a conventional job, and learned some things about maintaining a healthy relationship. With that relative stability and sanity established, I found myself drawn back to my interest in Buddhism.

In a sense, I was finding my way back to myself. Early in my sobriety I simply did what I was told and checked the boxes of the Steps: Powerless? For sure. Higher Power? Why not? Inventory? Gotta do it. Amends? Let's go. Carry the message? What a joy! But as confidence in my own recovery developed, and my intellectual life grew deeper, I found that this traditional approach to recovery didn't completely fit who I was becoming. First there was the problem of God. While I wasn't a confirmed atheist, I also was not a Christian, or for that matter, a theist. I related much more to Buddhism which sees monotheism as a human construction, and essentially irrelevant in addressing the question of suffering. No matter how much I believe or pray, I'm still subject to sickness, old age, and death. No God can eliminate greed, hatred, and delusion. Whether there is or isn't a God simply didn't matter to me.

As for inventory, I saw how valuable it was, but at times I felt that the focus on "character defects" and "shortcomings" spun me in negative ways, ways that triggered depressive and self-abnegating thinking. I knew I needed to stay current with my behavior, but persistently writing down all my failings didn't seem like the most helpful way to do that. With these concerns and questions, I started to ask myself how I wanted my program to look. Could the Buddhist practice and teachings intersect with the Twelve Steps and resonate more deeply for me?

And so it was that my program and my meditation practice evolved and merged so that meditation is now part of the entire Step process for me. And it's not just that meditation helps me with the Steps; the Steps also help me with meditation. I'm going to take you through the Steps and show you how meditation can be applied to that entire process. But first, I want to talk about how recovery lays a foundation for meditation.

In my early years of practice, as I've described, I wasn't sober. Though I was practicing meditation, I wasn't practicing sila, the moral foundation of Buddhist teachings. Without sila, developing peace and insight in meditation is difficult. If you are acting unskillfully in your life—
selfishly, harmfully, addictively—you probably aren't feeling calm. You might be living with guilt and remorse or fear of being found out. Your relationships are likely fraught. And sila isn't just actions; it's also thoughts and attitudes. If you think getting loaded is the way to happiness, even when you aren't loaded, that belief is influencing your mind, your moods, your behavior, your whole life. So, sila is an attitude that says, "Being sober and living with honesty, kindness, and seeking wisdom is my path." That way, even if you stray a bit, you are pointed in the right direction.

When we get sober and come into recovery, we don't just give up addictive behavior. We also stop lying, cheating, and stealing. Our sexual behavior becomes more wholesome, less selfish. (In fact, if we give up drinking and drugging and don't change our other behavior in this way, I'd go so far as to say that we aren't really in recovery.) This is one reason I like teaching meditation to people in recovery: they already

Sought Through Meditation

have a foundation of sila. If they've written an inventory and made amends, they also don't have a lot of skeletons in the closet that might come out as their meditation taps into underlying tendencies. Now you are living skillfully and also being guided by wise intentions. You are on a positive, spiritual path. So, this is how Step work and recovery support meditation.

Let me now talk about how meditation can be applied to the Twelve Steps.

Step One: The powerlessness and unmanageability described in Step One correlates directly to working with thoughts, feelings, and even the body in meditation. When we start sitting, we learn very quickly that we can't control our thoughts, that we are powerless over them and, indeed, of our mind. As with our addiction, this powerlessness doesn't mean we can't do anything about it. Two things happen: first, we change our relationship to our thoughts. And second, things start to calm down.

The way we change our relationship to thoughts is that we start to see them as objects of mind, rather than manifestations of "me." We see how conditioned they are, how depending upon moods and circumstances they vary greatly. We see how untethered from reality they can be, flitting from one idea to another, often irrationally. As we learn about Buddhism, we start to see how they fit into the model of "greed, hatred, and delusion" that the Buddha laid out. What that means is that we realize that what seems personal to me is actually much more universal. My thoughts aren't really different from anyone else's. They are driven by the same human impulses for comfort, safety, and control.

As these insights come to us with meditation, we realize that the wise relationship with all this noise in our head is not to fight it—which is just more "hatred"—but to accept it. Let it come and go. Our developing insight into impermanence reminds us that they will all pass if we just leave them alone.

This acceptance, then, has a quality of serenity in it, just as the "Serenity Prayer" implies. Out of this serenity, calming of the mind evolves quite naturally. We don't have to suppress thoughts or force the attention to stay with the breath. We simply take this new attitude towards our thoughts and wait. Just sit and trust in the process. Of course, we aren't just waiting, we are also watching, practicing mindfulness.

The stance we take with mindfulness, that quality of watching, is impersonal, and expresses the insight into not-self. In this way, this first step in meditation already holds the three key insights of Buddhism: impermanence, unsatisfactoriness, and selflessness. The thoughts that arise keep changing. They don't give us what we want. And they don't belong to us.

If we sustain our meditation, especially on retreats, we also discover our powerlessness over our body. If you sit still long enough it will start to hurt. As with the mind, we approach this with care, acceptance, and interest. Instead of trying to automatically fix it, to move or make ourselves more comfortable, we explore the sensations, investigating them as we do with thoughts. And in that investigation we see the same impermanence, unsatisfactoriness, and selflessness. As we learn to work with that, with the breath, with mindfulness, with calm, with receptivity, our relationship to the body changes as well.

Finally, Step One reminds us of our powerlessness over feelings and emotions. As we meditate feelings will come and go, and so we bring an attitude of investigation and acceptance. Not running from the painful or grasping onto the pleasant; seeing how they don't define us or belong to us. Learning to hold our feelings in this way can be one of the most valuable things we develop in meditation.

Step Two: Here the Higher Power idea is introduced to the Steps, so we need a way of translating that to Buddhism, and then to meditation. This is a question I've addressed throughout my writing, especially in my book *Buddhism & the Twelve Steps: HIGHER POWER* (originally published as *A Burning Desire*). My essential premise is that the Dharma is powerful and can take the place of a Higher Power in the Steps. Mindfulness, loving kindness, concentration, compassion, insight, faith, and many other aspects of the Buddhist path have great power, if we draw upon them. At the root of this is the Law of Karma which says that actions have results. This refers not just to behavior, but to thoughts as well, since thinking has karmic consequences. Once we realize this, that everything we think, say, or do has an impact on our life, we want to be careful what karma we are creating. We see how powerful these forces are. This then points us back to mindfulness, which is where we can observe thoughts and bring more wise attention to words and actions.

Returning to the Step, which says we "came to believe that a Power greater than ourselves could restore us to sanity," we can see how meditation applies to this. The powers we engage in meditation—mindfulness, loving kindness, effort, concentration, and others—are what dispel delusion, which is another word for insanity. Thus, when we trust in the Buddhist meditation path, we are expressing our belief in a Higher Power. This Power doesn't take the form of a God, but nonetheless, serves the same purpose. When we sit down to meditate, we bring our faith and confidence to that process. Even when it's challenging or when nothing seems to be happening, we persist because we believe in its efficacy. There is a quality of devotion that develops as we continue this path. When we meditate there is an element of surrender, just as there is on a faith-based religious path.

In Buddhism, this surrender focuses on the Three Refuges, Buddha, Dharma, and Sangha. While the Dharma provides the framework, the Buddha is our inspiration. His life, his example, and the principle of awakening that he represents give us a focus for our devotion. The Sangha, the community that has kept the teachings alive and carries them forward, supports us and gives us a spiritual home.

In practical terms, the way we apply this Step to our meditation is firstly in our persistence, meditating regularly. Secondly, as we sit, because we trust in the power of the Dharma, we work with whatever comes up, not running from the challenges. We will see such challenges dissolve under the light of mindfulness, concentration, loving kindness, and effort. And so our faith in the practice and in the Dharma will continue to grow.

Step Three: In meditation, "turning your will and your life over" is about fully committing to the process. It's easy to fall into resistance to what arises when meditating. Some pain in the body makes you decide to get up; a flood of thoughts makes it seem pointless to sit there. Sleepiness or restlessness makes it so unpleasant that you're not willing to keep going. Doubt about the whole project or your own capacity to carry it out takes you over. Any one or more of these or similar experiences can undermine your commitment to meditation. It takes real determination to sit through the barrage of challenges that come up when we practice.

Turning our "will" over means that we align ourselves with Right Intention. This means our focus is letting go and being kind. In meditation, these are key. In fact, these two aspects of practice more or less sum up the whole process. We learn to let go of desire and aversion; of fantasies and memories; of painful emotions and even pleasant mind states. Letting go means we aren't grasping after results in meditation nor clinging to concentration or other positive outcomes.

Kindness starts with ourselves. We don't react to the thoughts and feelings that arise with judgment or self-hatred. We bring an attitude of compassion to our experiences.

Turning our "life" over is showing up. Even if we'd rather be doing something else, we put in the time and effort each day. Meditation is our North Star, our guiding principle. It becomes like food or water to us, vital to our survival and health.

The "care" referred to in this Step is the benefit we derive from sticking with it. While many things may happen in our meditation, either pleasant or otherwise, at the end of the day—and often by the end of a sitting—we feel better, more calm, peaceful, and clear. The power of mindfulness, concentration, kindness, patience, and effort reward everything that we put into their cultivation.

Again, the Three Refuges offer us an alternative way of thinking about the devotional aspect of this Step. We understand and trust in the power of the Buddha, Dharma, and Sangha, resolving to live in accordance with the ideals, teachings, and community they embody. As one teacher puts it, "The Dharma takes care of those who take care of the Dharma."

Meditating is a surrender. Surrendering to reality, to the truth of our hearts and minds, of our bodies, our moods, our thoughts. We let it all wash over us without running. That surrender is the essence of Step Three.

Step Four: The traditional inventory prompted by the fourth Step is one of the most challenging aspects of the whole Twelve Step process. While nothing like it is implied in Buddhist teachings, over the years Western teachers have embraced something they call a "life review" for people on longer retreats. This seems to have evolved out of their recognition that many people on longer retreats found themselves going back over events of their lives, especially mistakes and regrets. While traditional Buddhist practice suggests that we should let go of such thoughts, the persistence of these challenging memories in so many students convinced Western teachers to take a different tack and guide people to work through such a review in a skillful way. After exploring this process, a student could then be guided back to the present and into ways of holding such memories in useful ways.

The origins of this adaptation may go back to Stephen Levine's book *A Year to Live*. As part of a reflection on death, Levine suggested taking time to reflect on our past, bringing gratitude and forgiveness to the process. That book and the practice it outlines has become the template for courses that are now offered by many Buddhist centers and teachers. And clearly, the life review has its parallel in the "searching and fearless moral inventory" of Step Four. (In fact, I've often wondered if Levine was inspired by that Step in writing his book.)

For myself, the role of meditation in inventory work is layered. First of all, meditation brings a clarity to memory that supports the inventory. Memories tend to bubble up out of meditative states, bringing material to the fore. In daily practice it's probably more accurate to connect these thoughts and images with Step Ten than Step Four. That Step is more immediate, more about present-moment issues than the historical material of the fourth Step. Either way, we can make the case that meditation has a valuable role to play in the inventory process.

Let's talk about the mechanics of that role. When we sit, as I've said, thoughts and memories will come up unbidden. While our general task is to notice and let go of these thoughts, some will be more persistent or impactful than others. If we find such thoughts intruding over and over, it may be that they need more attention and care. This is where, instead of simply returning to the breath, we take time to explore both the content and the emotional impact of these thoughts. During meditation, what we're trying to do is make peace with these thoughts. As Levine suggests, forgiveness may come into play, forgiveness of others or forgiveness of ourselves—or asking for forgiveness from others. We want to respond with compassion, with love, and ultimately equanimity. This last quality is what fosters serenity, peace.

Bringing mindfulness to the inventory process helps us

hold it with kindness and balance. This answers the key challenge of taking our own measure, how we address all the difficult memories from the past and feelings in the present that come up. Meditation can give us the space and clarity to be open and honest with ourselves without creating more suffering.

We can also think of certain standard Buddhist reflections as inventories. First of these is noticing when one of the five hindrances is present. Here we bring mindfulness to these challenging qualities. We explore the underlying longings and resistance; the self-centered beliefs and biased judgments; the conditioned and habitual patterns of unwholesome thought. In this way we take a present-moment inventory of our mind state. This suggests that any moment of mindfulness is a moment of inventory, and that is true.

And so, taking note of whatever is appearing in the mind, whether pleasant, unpleasant, or neutral is a sort of inventory. Tracking effort and energy. Observing pleasant states like calm and joy. Connecting with emotions and mind states. Indeed the whole mindfulness meditative process is "searching and fearless" and requires a level of honesty and truthful self-evaluation that fits perfectly with the Twelve Step process.

Step Five: The central idea of Step Five "admitting to another human being." In silent meditation, this isn't something we can do. But the Step tells us to first admit to God and ourselves. Since I don't believe in an external or intervening God, I use this idea as a push to be absolutely honest with myself. Along with this honesty about the "exact nature" of my mistakes or failings, I bring compassion, forgiveness, wisdom, and kindness. Without those qualities my inventory will wind up being a form of self-flagellation, a recitation of how "bad" I am, which only sends me into more unwholesome states. This serves no purpose. And so, the honesty and admissions of Step Five always need to be held in this broad space, recognizing that all humans make mistakes. We can only try to correct those and move forward in wise and skillful ways.

As for the "admitting" part of the Step, one source of support is a Buddhist teacher. Whether on retreat, in a community gathering, or a one-to-one conversation it's valuable to get guidance from a trained meditation teacher or monastic. While reading and listening to instruction on meditation is helpful, there is nothing like working with someone directly to help us gain clarity about our practice.

Step Six: Because of its theistic language, this is another Step that takes a complete reframing In Buddhist terms. We can see it as the groundwork for letting go, for changing. This is essentially what our whole practice is about. We show up and apply the tools of meditation as best we can and trust the process to unfold in a beneficial way.

The idea that we need to be "ready" to change or to let go points us to resistance. Everyone says they want to be happier or healthier or more peaceful, but when faced with the tasks involved, people often balk. Putting in the work is very different from wanting or hoping for change. This is as true in the realm of addiction and recovery as it is in Buddhist meditation.

In terms of our practice, then, this is a place where we can examine our willingness to do the work. Do we avoid sitting? Are we afraid to go deeper, take a retreat or study with a teacher? What are we still holding on to? Here we have the opportunity to challenge ourselves, to cut through the fear and move forward.

Step Seven: I've long viewed this Step as the crux of recovery and of Dharma practice. Essentially, this is the Step where we let go, and that is the key to recovery and to Buddhism. First, we let go of our addictive behavior; then we let go of our unwholesome qualities, the so-called "character defects" and "shortcomings." That's the Twelve Step work. The work of Buddhist practice picks up there, going deeper into letting go. This aims at abandoning craving and self-view all together, admittedly ideals few will attain, but nonetheless, important guides for Dharma practice.

The late Buddhadasa Bhikkhu, a legendary Thai Forest monk, says that from a Buddhist view, "asking God" means we "beseech the Law of Karma through our action." In Buddhism, "action" refers not just to deeds, but thoughts and words as well. Thus, our effort to change, to let go, to "remove our shortcomings," depends upon changing how we think. This can only happen if we are aware of what we are thinking.

Here's where our meditation becomes so important. Discerning whether we are thinking skillfully or unskillfully, wisely or unwisely, requires clear attention, mindfulness. Without that we simply keep acting on past conditioning. This automatic pilot is mostly driven by underlying tendencies of craving, aversion, and confusion. In this way, we keep making poor choices and acting out addictive habits, as our life careens from one catastrophe to another.

When we cultivate the Noble Eightfold Path, we change the thrust of our life, just as the Steps themselves put us on another track. Bringing the wisdom, clarity, and integrity of this Path into our life changes everything. Now we can interrupt unwholesome habits of mind, of speech, and of action. Mindfulness is at the heart of this process. However, every element of the Eightfold Path plays a vital part. (See Appendix I for more on the Eightfold Path.)

Step Eight: With this Step we begin the amends process by making a list of those we harmed. The quiet of meditation has a way of bringing forward memories that were long forgotten and people we thought we had left far behind.

Again, this Step challenges us to be ready. As we reflect on our list, we often discover that some amends are easier to face than others. Here in our meditation, we see, feel, and breathe with the fear and resistance that comes up regarding difficult amends. Let those feelings come through. Recognize that this is the result of your own mistakes. It is the fruit of your own karma. Are you willing to take responsibility for that? It's also helpful to recognize that putting someone on this list, and being willing to make amends to them doesn't mean that you have to make amends to them. Remember to keep Steps Eight and Nine separate. Here, just work with willingness. You can make a decision about the actual amends later.

Step Nine: We can't execute the practical elements of this Step in meditation, but there are other ways our meditation practice can utilize Step Nine. First is in making amends to ourselves. Just by establishing a meditation practice you are helping yourself to heal from the pain and trauma of addiction. When it comes to the harm we did in our addiction, much of it was to ourselves, and so our amends need to consider that. It was our bodies and minds that suffered from every unskillful action, even as we hurt others along the way. Practicing loving kindness, self-compassion, and forgiveness are direct ways that we can make meditative amends.

These Heart Practices can also be applied to the greater amends process. First of all, when preparing to make amends, it's good to cultivate a state of caring and acceptance. We never know how our words will be received, so we want to be ready for whatever comes back at us. There may be anger or refusal to accept our amends. There may be tears. There may be a warm receptivity. If we come into that moment with an open, loving heart we'll be able to work with whatever happens.

Another area where these practices can help with amends

is in the case of people who have died or disappeared from our life. If there's no possibility of making direct amends, then loving kindness and compassion meditation are ways to bring some healing and closure to those painful memories.

Reflecting on forgiveness opens another door for healing. Formal forgiveness practices address three aspects: asking forgiveness, offering forgiveness to others, and offering forgiveness to ourselves. (See "Guided Meditations")
Please note: It is always wise to discuss your planned amends with a sponsor or other trusted advisor before embarking on this challenging and sometimes risky process.
Step Ten: While essentially a reiteration of Steps Four through Nine, this Step is more specifically focused on the present moment or the present day. In that way, it parallels mindfulness meditation itself. Here we highlight the specific unwholesome or unhelpful qualities that are arising as we sit. As we see them, our intention is to let them go. This intention doesn't mean that we always succeed at this effort. That means we need to again bring acceptance and kindness to whatever we encounter in our meditation.

The Twelve Steps primarily address our harmful behaviors and qualities, as we must do in order to overcome an addiction. Much of meditation does the same. However, as part of our "meditative inventory," it's important to also highlight the wholesome and beneficial states that arise. Meditation isn't just about seeing the negative. Many positive experiences can happen as we meditate, and these should also be developed and acknowledged. Calm and serenity; joy and happiness; love, compassion, and equanimity are just some of these qualities. Take pleasure in such experiences.
Step Eleven: Here is where the Twelve Steps inform our meditation, rather than the other way around. The words of the Step can support our practice. First of these is "sought." The

implication and reminder are that we are seeking after something, and this means we are in process. We don't expect to arrive at a conclusion or finish the work we are engaged in, but rather see ourselves as on an open-ended path. The value of this reflection is that it helps us to let go of chasing goals. This then helps us to stay in the present moment with whatever is arising.

To "improve conscious contact," points to our effort to be more present, to consciously contact our body and mind right now. This is another way of saying, "be mindful."

"Knowledge of His will," stripped of its theistic context can simply point to the growing clarity and wisdom that come out of meditation, what's called "insight" in the Buddhist tradition. It is this understanding that is truly transformative. While our practice can bring more calm and reduce stress, insight is what changes our whole understanding of ourselves, of our lives, and of the world. From those insights come different emotional reactions, different ways of seeing things, and different behaviors in response to those new ways of experiencing the world.

"The power to carry that out" is what comes out of transformative insight. Now we are living the insights, not just thinking about them. We've moved beyond an intellectual understanding into something transcendent.

Step Twelve: Spiritual awakening means different things to different people, and has different meanings in different religions and philosophies. Buddhism talks about "enlightenment." Even the different Buddhist traditions have their own definitions of this. But perhaps the most succinct is found in the Metta Sutta, the Buddha's teaching on loving kindness: "The pure hearted one, having clarity of vision, being freed from all sense desires, is not born again into this world." A

Sought Through Meditation

pure heart, clear seeing, non-clinging, and non-ego. These are the qualities of a spiritual awakening. When we meditate we cultivate these qualities and bring awareness to their arising. A "perfectly enlightened" one might always manifest them, but most of us simply experience them for moments at a time.

When we sense the transformation—the spiritual awakening—that our recovery and our practice has brought us, we naturally want to share that. In Buddhism, the formal way to do that is to "share the merit." The idea is that you offer the universe or all beings all the good things that you've attained. You give it away. This accords with the Buddhist principle of non-clinging, of not trying to hold on to things.

While this may be just a thought, it nonetheless, helps shift our perspective toward generosity and away from self-seeking. Meditation is such an intensely private experience that when good things start to happen, it's easy to think they are about "me." We can get caught in trying to hold on to or replicate meditative experiences. Sharing the merit is an antidote to this tendency.

The intention expressed by sharing the merit is compassion. This quality of caring about the suffering of others naturally opens in us as we go deeper in meditation. As we see more clearly how suffering arises and how it ends, we realize that what seems personal—our inner life and challenges—is actually universal. All beings suffer. All beings are subject to craving. This realization naturally triggers the heart-opening that leads to compassion. While there are formal ways of cultivating and sustaining this quality, mindfulness practice itself will often arouse it spontaneously.

This Step also reminds us in its final line to take the practice into the world after the bell rings. Meditation isn't an end in itself. To truly fulfill its mission, we must "practice these principles in all our affairs." Spiritual awakening only has true benefit when we share it in the world.

Heart Practices

The practice of mindfulness, while powerful and potentially transformative, can also become somewhat dry or mechanical. Further, the application of mindfulness alone to the difficult states that arise can be limited in its benefit. The practices and attitudes cultivated with what we call "heart practice" are the perfect complement to mindfulness meditation.

Traditionally called "Brahmaviharas," or "Divine Abodes," there are four aspects of heart practice:
- Loving kindness – the wish for yourself and others to be happy.
- Compassion – the wish for yourself and others to be free of suffering.
- Sympathetic/Appreciative Joy – taking joy in the happiness of others and the goodness around us.
- Equanimity – a balanced, peaceful state of mind that neither grasps at pleasure nor recoils from discomfort. A state of acceptance.

These qualities can be developed through specific meditation practices, and they can also be cultivated as attitudes to bring to our practice and our daily lives.

Loving kindness: The first of the Brahmaviharas and the key one, loving kindness, or metta in Pali, focuses on developing love toward ourselves and others. It is a quality and attitude we can cultivate to counter resentment and anger as well as negative self-talk. When we meditate, removing ourselves from distractions and activities, the mind is unleashed. Our practice attempts to rein in this wildness, training the mind to behave more helpfully and wisely. However, the destructive and hurtful qualities that are part of our conditioning can sometimes overwhelm our ability to manage them through mindfulness alone. Metta gives us a tool for responding to those states.

Metta begins with the reflection that everyone wants to be happy. And that includes us. With this idea in mind, we observe how many of our own thoughts and behaviors, as well as those of other people, run in the opposite direction, toward stress, conflict, agitation, and worry. In the Buddha's words: "sorrow, lamentation, pain, grief, and despair." This insight, into the counterproductive behavior of humans inspires us to look for another way: loving kindness.

When mindfulness reveals to us the harmful movements of mind, we apply the practice and reflections of loving kindness. This is the practice I described earlier called "replacing." Here we intentionally bring a positive thought or feeling to mind in order to weaken or displace a negative one. In formal metta practice, we often use phrases like "May you be happy," and "May I be happy." You can also visualize loved ones to evoke feelings of care and kindness, or learn to feel your way into that state using the breath and a gentle inclination of the heart.

Initially when learning loving kindness meditation, we simply try to learn what it feels like to arouse metta. With time this becomes a familiar state that, like mindfulness, can be brought to the fore with a moment's reflection. Then it becomes part of our spiritual toolbox, something we call upon quite naturally when needed.

Key to the development of metta in this regard is learning to feel metta for ourselves. For many people this can be the most difficult aspect of the practice. Many people—especially those in recovery—struggle with negative feelings of self-worth. The idea of loving yourself can seem daunting. I recommend that you take as much time as you need to cultivate this aspect of your meditation. Letting go of self-hatred and becoming comfortable in your own skin is one of the most important steps we can take in our spiritual growth.

A key to developing metta for ourselves is the universal aspect of the practice. It points to the fact that everyone wants happiness, and yet most of us do the exact opposite of what will bring that. Instead of letting go, we cling; instead of loving, we resent; instead of paying attention, we space out. The point is that you are not uniquely flawed. Everyone makes these mistakes. That doesn't make us unworthy of love. In fact, it makes us more in need of love. If we can just see ourselves as one of the multitude of humans trying to find our way in this troubled world, perhaps we can bring an attitude of kindness to ourselves.

(My book *Living Kindness* explores these teachings more deeply.)

Compassion: While metta offers happiness to all beings, compassion, or karuna, focuses specifically on those who are suffering. Again, this includes ourselves. The challenge of compassion is that it requires us to become more aware of suffering. Many people want to look away from the pain and distress of the world, but the Buddha insists that we be present for the suffering of others and ourselves. Without this honest engagement, no real healing can take place. If we are always trying to avoid or ignore suffering, we put ourselves in conflict with reality, an unsustainable stance. Anyone who has successfully dealt with their own addiction understands that denying their pain only leads to deepening their misery.

The path of mindfulness and compassion points to another way. As we practice meditation and tune into our own suffering, we learn to bring a quality of care to that distress. The Buddhist teachings on compassion encourage us to see how all beings are subject to suffering, mental and physical, and that the wise response to that is compassion, kindness. One of the outgrowths of mindfulness meditation is to begin to see our experience as less personal, more universal. As the mind quiets and the heart opens, we understand that in essence we are not different from others, that what we feel is what others feel. As the Four Noble Truths become clearer, we see that each of us is complicit in our own suffering and that we perpetuate that pain through our ignorance, through not seeing our role in its manifestation. This insight arouses the motivation to serve and heal others in the world. In meditation it elicits kindness for our own suffering as well as the wish for others to be free. It is this process of deepening insight into the human condition that underlies the Buddhist focus on suffering and transforms our relationship to our own pain and that of others.

In practice, self-compassion might play out like this: A negative thought about yourself arises and you recognize it. You become aware of the pain that the thought is causing you. Instead of doubling down with more thoughts, you bring compassion to yourself. You briefly reflect that you wish to be free from suffering and that this thought is causing suffering. You take an attitude of kindness toward yourself. Then you simply return to your breath.

Such a process doesn't exclude the idea that there might be something you've done or some personal pattern that needs to be addressed. No one is perfect. It simply means that berating ourselves for our failures is not a productive way to address any shortcomings. In the same way that we train a dog with rewards, not punishments, our own training is more productive when done with kindness.

The book *Self-Compassion* by Kristin Neff is a great guide

to this practice.

Sympathetic Joy: The third Brahmavihara, mudita, or Sympathetic Joy is perhaps the most obscure one. The idea that we can derive happiness from the successes and joys of others isn't something that is immediately apparent. And yet, when we reflect on our lives, we find that when friends or family bring good news, it certainly tends to brighten our own mood. Mudita suggests we should actively seek out such moments.

Once we understand the concept, we will start to see the pleasure we take in seeing a baby laughing, a puppy pulling on its leash, or a young couple holding hands and smiling. The trick is to let yourself be immersed in such simple moments, to bring awareness to the joy.

As a meditative process, mudita is practiced by bringing to mind people we know and imagining them doing things they love. See them as happy, beaming, taking joy in some activity. You can also evoke mudita by reflecting on the happiness that people are experiencing. Remembering a friend's recent promotion; reflecting on a niece's graduation; bringing to mind a neighbor's pride in a new garden.

Mudita, like the other Brahmaviharas, is as much an attitude as an experience. To develop this attitude, we first need to understand what gets in the way of sympathetic joy. Qualities like envy, comparing, and striving for position put us in conflict with other people's happiness. We see life as a zero-sum game whereby anytime someone else gets something we are losing. This is a narrow way of viewing things and creates more suffering. If instead of these self-centered attitudes we see that happiness is limitless and success helps everyone, we can make a shift. My first creative writing teacher addressed this when someone in the class got their book published. He suggested that instead of feeling jealous, we should realize that we were in a class with other really good writers and that we should take joy in being in such an environment. We were much more likely to achieve our own success by working with successful, talented people than otherwise.

The beautiful truth of mudita is that someone somewhere is always experiencing joy, and if we connect with that, we can always find a way of lifting our own spirits. While this obviously has limits, the idea that we can be happier by looking for happiness around us is certainly a beneficial attitude.

I want to bring in another aspect of practice here, that, while not the same as mudita, fits in. That is joy. People don't often associate meditation with joy, in the same way they don't associate recovery with joy. Nonetheless, it is a quality that can be cultivated in meditation, and in fact, naturally arises at some times when we are meditating. The Buddhist term "piti" points to a kind of energetic experience, uplifting, sometimes floaty or buzzy that can occur as the mind settles into tranquility. While it's not so helpful to go searching for this, when we start to get little inklings, we can bring those feelings to the fore as our main object of awareness. This then tends to evoke greater feelings of well-being and even rapture.

One way to incline the mind toward such experiences is simply to smile while meditating. Not so much a grin, but just curling up the corners of the mouth. This tends to brighten the mood and stimulate piti. The Gathas meditation mentioned above and described in the chapter "Guided Meditations" is a good way to do this.

Another way to arouse joy is to reflect on gratitude. To be alive, in recovery, on a spiritual path is a great gift. While we all struggle, it's important to remember all the goodness in our lives. (My book Recovering Joy explores this topic more broadly.)

Just remember, it's okay to be happy when you meditate.

Equanimity: Known as upekkha in Pali, the fourth Brahmaviha has a special role both in working with the heart practices and more generally in Buddhist meditation and philosophy. First of all, it is meant to balance the emotionality of the other practices. Loving kindness can lapse into passion or grasping as our longing for others to be happy sweeps us away. Compassion can become pity or overwhelm us with sorrow as we reflect on all the suffering in the world. Sympathetic joy can become a kind of frantic elation as we keep looking for happy people we can celebrate. Equanimity helps to moderate all these impulses.

The key reflection in this practice goes like this: "All beings are the owners of their karma. Their happiness or unhappiness depends upon their actions, not on my wishes for them." This is meant to remind us that simply repeating phrases in meditation isn't going to change someone else's life. This helps us to quell our grasping tendencies and the feeling of responsibility we might develop when reflecting on others and wishing them well.

Equanimity is often misunderstood to be a kind of dullness or passivity. In fact as a mind state, it is one of the most pleasant feelings one can experience. It is characterized by the lack of grasping or pushing away, desire and aversion. When these two qualities are absent, the feeling of peace is profound. We only need to look at the Four Noble Truths to understand why. The cause of suffering is these exact qualities, grasping and pushing away; the end of suffering is when they are abandoned. While the language of this teaching is cast in the negative, the end of suffering is the beginning of joy, of freedom, of serenity. What we are all seeking.

In some sense the first three Brahmaviharas fill us up with wholesome and joyful qualities. Then equanimity empties us. The paradox of this is that it is the filling up that allows us to let go in this deep and profound way. That is because metta, karuna, and mudita are healing energies that, when fulfilled leave us calm, open, and fearless. They deepen our concentration and help us to abandon the unwholesome tendencies that dog us. When these qualities come to fruition, it's a natural next step to let go into the deep serenity of upekkha.

Equanimity appears in other Dharma settings. It is the last of the Ten Paramis or Perfections; it is the fourth of the four jhanas, the deepest states of concentration; and it is the seventh of the Seven Factors of Enlightenment. In this last role, equanimity is taken to a profound level of letting go. The mind is deeply still even as it attunes to the rapid change called "anicca," or impermanence. Anicca when fully perceived reveals the unstable nature of reality. To see this reality is, in some way, to have our entire world view shattered. We see that everything we rely on is actually unreliable. Our body, our mind, those around us, the earth, the sky, the universe itself are all in radical flux. Only a mind incapable of disturbance can encounter this reality without fear or overwhelming displacement. This is the reason that concentration and equanimity are the final two elements of the Seven Factors, as they prepare us to face the deepest truth.

Part III: The Whole of Our Lives

Insight and Spiritual Awakening

Step Twelve tells us that among the results of working the Steps will be a "spiritual awakening." Many people come to meditation with hopes of such a transformation, sometimes imagining a magical world of bliss and detachment. But that's not what the Steps or the Dharma are promising.

I find it both useful and uplifting to consider spiritual awakening and insight in very broad terms. For me, waking up to my addictions and how they were undermining my happiness and spiritual growth was a huge and transformative moment. It changed the entire trajectory of my life. I can't find any more important moment in my spiritual life. So, to me, that is a spiritual awakening.

I find other awakenings throughout the Twelve Steps: waking up to my "defects," to the power of amends, and to trusting in the recovery process. When I realized how much easier it was to be honest about my failings, I felt a wonderful sense of freedom. There is so much letting go that can happen in recovery, and most of it comes down to ego, not feeling the need to protect, inflate, or degrade myself. All these experiences are insights and awakenings.

Buddhist insights tend to be less personal. They are largely about changing our perspective on reality. These center around three things that have come up repeatedly in this book: impermanence, unsatisfactoriness, and not-self.

The importance of insight into impermanence relates directly to our tendency to cling. Everything is in constant flux, but we keep trying to hold on. This puts us in conflict with reality and creates an unreconcilable tension. The more we remember the truth of impermanence, the less of this tension we experience.

The fact that things are constantly changing means no moment of satisfaction is sustainable. We are bound to be frustrated, unsatisfied, unless we let go of our craving for satisfaction.

According to the logic of the Buddha, if there is a "self," then it is something stable, abiding. However, because everything we point to as self—body, thoughts, feelings—is shifting and changing, none of those things can be "I, me, or mine." Instead, the interaction of all our body/mind processes creates an illusion that there is some center, some individual who is experiencing it all. When the mind becomes very steady in meditation, we can see how the "self" is being created moment-by-moment through these processes.

And so, insight into impermanence, unsatisfactoriness, and not-self frees us from the suffering that attachment causes. This spiritual awakening shifts our perspective on reality, breaking the spell that ordinarily controls us.

In the Twelve Step world, the problem of self is expressed differently. It's more about not being self-centered or selfish. Seeing that when our sole motivation is self-interest, we wind up alienating people and causing ourselves pain.

Meditation gives us a special look into our inner life. We are directly exposed to the processes by which we develop opinions, latch onto emotions, and try to control or influence the world with our minds. We see how we project good and bad events into the future. How we mull over past events with regrets, nostalgia, and guilt. We learn about our relationship to our body and to pain. We see how we create our own suffering. This is all grist for insight. If we understand and reflect wisely on what we see and experience, wisdom will grow. This is the great task of our meditation.

Sought Through Meditation

A few other reflections. These days a lot of people are turning to so-called "plant medicine," psychedelic substances, for a taste of spiritual awakening. As someone committed to sobriety, I avoid these drugs. Nonetheless, many wise people suggest that, when used properly, significant benefits can come from them. That may be true when they are used properly. And it is this question of proper use that becomes particularly thorny for addicts. We have such a tendency to chase pleasure and avoid pain, and to adopt behaviors habitually, that when we take a drug with the intention of working on our spiritual condition, it's easy for us to fall back into less wholesome intentions, to, in other words, trigger our addictive tendencies.

One way to avoid this is to only take such substances under strictly controlled circumstances. One of these might be a supervised clinical setting with professionals. Such settings are becoming more available. Here one isn't randomly popping a pill or mushrooms or peyote, but going through a strict protocol with clear controls. That doesn't mean there isn't still risk. Even the people who administer these treatments report that some people have harrowing experiences when under the effects of these powerful hallucinogens.

Another setting is a traditional, shaman-led ritual. Here one is being invited into an Indigenous culture's ancient spiritual path. Opportunities to take part in these rituals have become somewhat commercialized. You pay your money and you take your trip. Here, again, there can be significant psychic risks. Further, it can become another kind of hedonism that smacks of spiritual tourism. My understanding is that traditionally these drugs were only ingested at the end of a sometimes-years-long spiritual process. Like a Christian taking their first communion or a Jewish person having a Bar or

Bat Mitzvah, the actual ritual was the culmination of training in a religious system, not a one-off trip that is supposed to blow your mind (in a good way).

Much of the work today with these substances is focused on healing rather than spiritual awakening. Researchers are finding benefits for people suffering from PTSD, trauma, and, indeed, addiction, as well as other forms of mind/body suffering. Again, these results come in clinical settings, not self-administered doses. I believe that attempts to heal yourself from active addiction through using psychedelics on your own is unwise.

My advice is, take great care when approaching any of these drugs. Get very clear with yourself and with others about your intention. Talk to people you trust, a sponsor, therapist, teacher, or anyone else who has your best interest at heart. Remember, "spiritual awakening" isn't a onetime thing. It is the journey of our lives.

Teachers and Community

Meditation is an internal process. But that doesn't mean it's a solitary one. Without teachers and community, it's very hard to make progress, just as Twelve Step recovery depends upon meetings, sponsors, and group support.

The very first time I tried to meditate I failed miserably. I was on the road with a band, and I went to a local high school track to exercise. Afterward I opened the side door of my van and sat down. I read from a book by Alan Watts, then closed my eyes for what was probably less than a minute. I had no idea what I was doing and gave up in frustration. It wasn't until I took meditation instruction from a teacher a couple years later that I was able to get some understanding of the process. And throughout my years of practice I have depended upon teachers for guidance.

Most teachers are affiliated with one or another school of Buddhism, so their resonance for you will likely be directly tied to that tradition. Appendix II discusses these. Here I will simply say that my own path has been Theravada Buddhism, which in Western lay practice has transmuted into Insight Meditation. This thread of Buddhism is essentially the source of mindfulness meditation, which is now a broadly taught and practiced secular approach.

The role of a teacher in Buddhism is not the same as a sponsor in recovery. While you might develop a personal relationship with a teacher or work one-on-one, to a great extent it's not necessary to even know your teacher. The teacher functions as a conduit for Dharma, a guide and wise elder. There are some teachers I have never met who have had a great impact on my practice and my understanding of Dharma through their books and recordings. Others have become friends.

The thing is that our meditative, and indeed spiritual development is mostly dependent on our own actions. A teacher simply can't solve our problems for us, as much as we'd all like that. Nonetheless, to learn meditation, it's very helpful to work directly or indirectly with an experienced teacher. One of the most valuable ways to learn is to listen to a teacher answer other people's questions about meditation. In that way you can sit back and consider what's being said. There are many complex and at times confusing aspects to meditation. Hearing a teacher discuss these challenges can shed light on your own practice. Of course, you can ask your own questions as well.

These days the prevalence of apps, online courses, and videos might seem to have supplanted the need for teachers. However, there is nothing like being in the same space as someone. Here we pick up more than words or instructions. Teachers communicate with their presence as well as their words. While we can certainly learn in other ways, there is no replacement for encountering the Dharma in person.

The other valuable support along with teachers is community. As one of the "Three Jewels," "sangha" holds a special place in Buddhism. Just as recovery is so dependent on fellowship, so too, meditation is enhanced when we practice with a group. Just as it's hard to sustain sobriety alone, so too, sustaining a meditation practice is much easier with the support of a community.

When I started meditating all those years ago, there were very few teachers and meditation groups. That's one of the reasons that teacher training programs have proliferated, so that meditation could be offered in many more areas. Today, pretty much every urban area in the U.S., as well as many smaller communities have a qualified meditation teacher. I've also known people who, when they could find no local group, just started inviting friends to join them. They might meet once a week to meditate and perhaps read a book or listen to a talk together. Such intimate gatherings can be even more helpful than some of the larger groups that form around well-known teachers.

Whatever works for you, whatever resources are available for you, seek out a community of like-minded meditators. Your practice will thrive in that environment.

Retreats

The Buddha often refers to what he is teaching as a "training." We are training our minds. Modern research into the impacts of meditation suggest that we are in fact training our brains as well, establishing and strengthening neural pathways. These connections help develop stronger concentration and attentional capacity. We can make the simple comparison of training the body, going to the gym to strengthen muscles and increase flexibility. Intensive meditation retreats are the "gyms" of the mind.

In the Insight Meditation tradition retreats are modeled on a semi-monastic form. The idea is to practice continuous mindfulness with as few distractions as possible. You practice "Noble Silence," which means that you only speak during the occasional meetings with a teacher and perhaps when there is an opportunity to ask questions. The quiet and simplicity allow you to sink deeply into meditation.

Retreats can run for as short as one day or as long as three months. (In the Tibetan tradition there is a three-year retreat, but this is a different form from Insight Meditation, and has a large study component.). A typical retreat is five to ten days. That usually gives you time to "settle in," and experience some depth in practice.

As you can imagine (or know if you've been on retreat), the beginning stages—the first day or more—of silence and continuous meditation can be especially challenging. Going from our ordinary busy lives to the quiet and stillness of intensive practice takes adjustment time. Typically you seesaw from dull, sleepiness to restless agitation. It can feel as if all the stress of our life is catching up with us and we could sleep for a month. At other times we're just waiting for the bell to ring in the meditation hall because we can't stand to sit there another minute longer.

All of this passes, and when it does, we start to encounter the deeper and broader aspects of meditation. As tranquility develops a subtle pleasure may arise. We begin to see the workings of the mind and the formation of thoughts, as our mental activity becomes clearer. We develop a sensitivity to the body that reveals levels of experience never encountered before.

Outside of sitting, in walking meditation and ordinary activities like eating, washing, or doing other tasks, we bring mindfulness to bear in ways that open up our understanding of our minds and of the Dharma. We seem to enter into another, deeper reality.

What comes out of all this is certainly a more sophisticated understanding of meditation and an increased ability to work with all that happens in practice. The greatest value, though, are the insights that arise and become clear through this intensive work. It's not so much that we have some sudden revelation (although that can happen), but rather that we start to intuitively view and respond to the world and its stimuli in wiser ways. Buddhist teachings that might have been intriguing before, now resonate directly with our experience. We don't just understand, we know.

On a practical level, the training of neural pathways makes it easier and more pleasant to meditate going forward. While the deep serenity of a retreat might fade after coming home, the base level of our meditation will rise if we sustain a daily practice. For most people, such growth can only come with this intensive training. That gives it a special value.

I need to acknowledge that the practical issues of going on retreat, namely taking time away from work and/or family, and the financial cost make it difficult for many people to embark on this training. While I can't solve that problem for anyone, I can suggest that if you are really interested in taking your practice to this next level, plan ahead. Many retreats are scheduled a year or more in advance, so that gives you plenty of time to make arrangements if possible. Also, many centers offer scholarships and discounts of various types that are worth looking into. While it's never comfortable asking for help, the spirit of the Dharma is generosity, so don't be afraid to reach out. Those who offer these teachings tend to be kind and understanding. They love to see people inspired by the Dharma and want to make it easy for people to access these teachings.

Daily Practice

The first hurdle in becoming a meditator is showing up, just as it is for sobriety. Many people tell me that they "want" to start meditating but don't have the discipline. Or they can't find the time. Or they can't sit still. Or they think too much. Or they always fall asleep. I'm sure you see where I'm going with this. We put up roadblocks for ourselves. But we're the ones that put them up, so we're the only ones who can pull them down.

First of all, discipline. I don't love that word because it sounds unpleasant, like I have to force myself to do something. With meditation, I think of it more like taking a shower. In fact, I once heard a Korean Zen Master say, "We clean our bodies every day, but where do we clean our minds?" I always feel better after a shower. And after meditating. What I'm getting at is that how we think about meditation can help us to develop a regular practice.

The simplest way to establish a daily practice is to schedule it into your day. You can literally put it on your calendar, or simply plan your day to have space for sitting. This is best done in the morning before work and before your day gets too busy. Some people like to drink some coffee or tea before meditating, while others are happy to get up and sit. For myself, I find that a shower wakes me up enough to meditate, while caffeine tends to make my mind too busy. Experiment with what works for you energetically.

Another way to commit to daily practice is to say that no matter how your day goes, you're doing to sit down and follow the breath at some point, even if it's only for three breaths. In that way, on those days when things get away from you, you've still stuck with your commitment. And that commitment is key to the development of your practice.

A couple other thoughts. It's helpful, if possible, to have a space in your home dedicated to meditation. Even if it's just a corner of a room, this serves as a sacred space. When you see it you are reminded to practice. When you sit there, you are naturally drawn to meditate. You might keep a spiritual book or two there for reading after meditation, and you can also set up an altar of sorts. Here you might put special objects, photos of teachers, a Buddha statue, or anything else that helps you connect with your deeper self.

Daily practice doesn't just mean daily meditation, though. With mindfulness, we are trying to apply these teachings to all our activities to the best of our ability. Whether working, cleaning the house, riding a subway, or driving a car; taking a walk, going to the gym, or talking to a neighbor. Anything we do can be done with mindfulness. Mindfulness of the body is especially helpful and simple to apply. Just be aware of your feet when walking, your breath, any sensations.

An endlessly useful tool is mindful breathing. To stop at any moment in our day and take one or more mindful breaths is a simple and effective way to wake up. That action can reset your mind. When you are committed to a spiritual and wholesome way of living, sometimes all you need is a gentle reminder, something that breaks the momentum of stress that can often have us rushing through our day. You don't have to sit down or do anything special. In the middle of a business meeting, a conversation with a friend, shopping, gardening, or any other ordinary activity, the breath is always there. All you have to do is become aware of it, slipping from the stream of thoughts, words, and actions into an inner awareness for a moment. No one else even has to know you're doing it.

Mindfulness of the breath and the body often lead naturally to mindfulness of emotions. In terms of having a happy and comfortable life, there is perhaps no more important element of mindfulness practice than this. Even more subtle than thoughts, emotions run like a stream underneath perception. Our sense of who we are and the quality of our life is more or less defined by these feelings. While we can cultivate insight and a wiser relationship to our emotions in meditation, as shown in the section "Changing Our Relationship to Difficult Emotions," navigating our inner world in our daily lives is even more important. Certain ideas and practices support this.

First is the recognition of impermanence. Emotions often feel solid, as if we are stuck with them. And that feeling can trigger other feelings and attitudes. We wind up thinking about our emotions, judging them, trying to fix them or figure out how to change them. This then tends to actually reinforce the feelings. Just thinking about depression, for instance, is kind of depressing. Thinking about anxiety can make you more anxious. Instead, mindfulness, as always, says, just feel the feeling. In that process, remembering that the feeling won't last long really helps. Otherwise it can seem as if we are going to be feeling this unpleasant feeling forever. What we discover is that if we don't reinforce the feelings with more rumination, they tend to fade pretty quickly. Again, we can do this work in the midst of our day. A feeling comes up; we take a few breaths as we let ourselves be present for the energy in the body. We remind ourselves that we're okay, that this is just a passing feeling, and we move on with our day.

As we learn to be more open and present to what we are feeling, we become less susceptible to emotional swings.

We aren't suppressing or trying to escape emotions, but by breathing with them and recognizing their impermanent and impersonal nature, we can ride them out without overreacting.

I acknowledge that for persistent or clinical conditions, this practice isn't always enough. For chronic emotional states, we need to turn to professionals for help at times. But I can tell you from personal experience, that this simple practice of mindfulness can help with a lot of the ordinary emotional challenges that arise in our daily lives.

See *The Mindful Way Through Depression* for more tips on dealing with difficult emotions.

Another important element to bring into daily practice is orienting toward kindness and compassion. Just as the heart practices help balance mindfulness in meditation, in our daily lives they serve the same function. This works both in how we relate to ourselves—our thoughts and feelings—and how we relate to others and the world around us.

We all make mistakes. Whether in our work or our personal lives, these moments can throw us, triggering negative self-talk and self-judgment. Learning to respond to these thoughts with kindness and self-compassion is an important part of integrating Dharma practice into our daily lives. This first requires that we are mindful of these thoughts as they appear, and then that we train ourselves to remember to bring an attitude of love and care to ourselves. It takes times to develop this orientation. I encourage you to practice loving kindness and compassion meditation and then reflect on their relationship to your real-life situations.

Incorporating the heart practices into our relationships with others and the greater world also plays an important role in daily practice. We try to remember that everyone struggles, everyone is subject to dukkha and deserving of love and compassion. Even when people are unskillful or hurt us, we can remember that they are acting out of their own confusion, "doing the best they can."

When we look at the wider world, through the news or political situation, we can also bring this broader perspective. In my book *Living Kindness*, I suggest we read the news as the "Greed, Hatred, and Delusion Report," a catalog of human failings that have ever been part of our world. We see history through the lens of the Four Noble Truths. When people don't develop wisdom, they are always driven by ignorance and craving, and thus creating suffering. This is the tragedy of human life, of history itself. The Dharma encourages us to view this all with great compassion. When we develop this attitude, it helps us navigate the difficult and painful realities that surround us.

Finally, insight into suffering inspires us to heal the world. When we integrate Buddhist teachings on mindfulness and compassion into our lives, we realize it's not enough to meditate on suffering. If we are to truly live the teachings, we are challenged to act. This can take many forms, but they all come down to one thing: service. Just as Step Twelve encourages us to help other addicts, as our Dharma practice matures, we are naturally drawn to caring for others and the world. I hope you will find some ways to live your practice in this joyful way.

Part IV: Guided Meditations

Getting Started

A written guided meditation isn't ideal. You can't read and meditate at the same time. For that reason, I've put recorded versions of all these meditations on my website. You can also study these guidelines and try to remember the instructions as you meditate. You could read them slowly and either reflect on the words or try to do one thing at a time. Or, finally, you could record the instructions yourself. The important thing is to meditate regularly.

A baseline time for practice is 20 minutes. If you can increase that over time, to 30 and eventually to 45 minutes, that will help you develop more concentration and stronger mindfulness. Don't turn this into a competition, but do see if you can stretch yourself a bit. Nonetheless, if you don't have much time, it's more important to sit daily than it is to hit some mark. Don't use the lack of time as an excuse not to practice. To listen to guided meditations, go to https://kevin-griffin.net/sought-through-meditation-guided-practices/

Standard Mindfulness Practice

Begin by establishing a stable posture, as I described in "The Practice" section above. Check your balance and alignment by tipping forward and back, then side to side. Settle into the posture that feels most grounded.

Take some time to scan through the body and release any tension you can. Relax the jaw. Open the chest. Soften the belly so that the breath can move deeply into the body.

Notice your mood and energy. Is there any prominent emotion present? Are you tired or restless? Just feel these feelings without trying to fix or change them. Relax and accept the mood and energy you are starting with.

Now begin to focus on the breath. Choose between the tip

of the nose and the belly as a focal point. If you follow the breath at the nostrils, you'll be feeling the sensations of air coming in and out. If you follow the breath at the belly, you're paying attention to the movement of the belly and diaphragm.

Try to sustain your attention on the breath. Follow the whole of the breath, from start to finish, in and out.

If you notice that your mind has wandered and you've lost touch with the breath, gently come back and start again, reconnecting with the sensations of breathing.

If your posture has slumped, very slowly bring yourself back into balance, using inhalations to bring the body up.

Continue with this process for the period of meditation. Don't worry about how many thoughts you have or how long you're able to stay with the breath. The important thing is to be consistent in practice. Results of practice will always fluctuate over time.

Noting

This is a variation of the standard mindfulness practice.
Begin by establishing your posture.
Do a brief body scan.
Connect with the breath.
If you are following the breath at the nostrils, start to make a mental note, "In, out," with each inhalation and exhalation. The words are soft, in the back of the mind. The breath is the primary focus.

When you notice that the mind has wandered, make a mental note, "Thinking, thinking," then gently return to the breath. Avoid any commentary or judgment about the thoughts. Just let go and come back.

If your attention is drawn to a sound, note, "Hearing, hearing," and return to the breath.

If your attention is drawn to a sensation in the body, note "Feeling, feeling," or "Sensation, sensation," and return to the breath.

Over time you can become more specific in identifying thoughts. You might notice thoughts like planning, remembering, judging; wanting, aversion, fear, or anger. Any of these can be noted, again, silently repeating, "Planning, planning," or whatever the type of thought is. Then returning to the breath. Don't worry about finding the exact right note. If no particular word comes to mind, just come back to the breath.

Because we're using language in this practice, there can be the tendency to go off into thinking about thinking. Be careful that the noting cuts off the thoughts and that you come right back to the simple experience of mindful breathing.

This practice can be applied to an entire period of meditation, or just brought in when it feels useful and dropped when it doesn't feel so helpful.

Sweeping

With Sweeping or Body Scan practice we move the attention through the body, little by little, focusing on any sensations we can feel. Typically this is done either head to feet or feet to head. If done very slowly, this can be stretched as long as forty-five minutes. It can also be done as a quick scan to bring the attention into the body as in the Standard Mindfulness Practice.

Begin by closing your eyes or just lowering your gaze and taking several mindful breaths. Have a sense of softening the body, letting the attention come to a general sense of awareness of sitting.

Now put the attention on the top of the head. Focus on a relatively small area a few inches around. Move the attention from the front to the back of the head, feeling any sensations. Be aware of temperature, solidity, pulsing, tingling, or any other feelings.

Move the attention down the left side of the head, the temple and the ears. Then down the right side.

Scan across the face: the forehead; the eyes; the nose; the cheeks, lips, and inside the mouth. Make sure your jaw is relaxed.

Move the attention down the neck and across the shoulders. Take the attention down the left arm little by little, the left hand; then the right arm and hand.

Explore the sensations in each hand, checking through each finger.

Now bring the attention to the chest, scanning across the chest, the armpits, and down to the belly.

Go to the back and slowly scan from top to bottom.

Feel the sensations in the groin, the hips, and buttocks.

Now scan down the left leg, thigh, knee, calf, shin, and ankle; then the right leg, thigh, knee, calf, shin, and ankle.

Move the attention over the left foot; and then over the right foot.

Now take a moment to see if you can feel the whole body at once, as a single object. Feel the energetic life of the body and its myriad sensations. Rest in that awareness.

Anapanasati – Mindfulness with Breathing

While mindful breathing is, in some ways, a generic form of meditation, Anapanasati is based on a specific teaching from the Buddha. There are four sections of this meditation, each of which has four instructions. It can be helpful to memorize the key words in these instructions so that you'll be able to guide yourself through the practice. I will use the words from the sutta to guide this meditation.

Note: At times when you work with this practice, all the states and experiences it points to won't be accessible to you. It is still helpful to utilize the teaching by reflecting on the words in the sutta, much as you do with Metta practice.

"Gone to the forest, to the root of a tree, to an empty hut..." Any quiet place will do.

"Fold the legs crosswise, and, set the body erect," Settle into your posture.

"Establishing mindfulness in front, ever mindful breathing in, ever mindful breathing out." Connect with the breath.

Mindfulness of Body

"Breathing in long, understand, 'I breathe in long.' Breathing out long, understand, 'I breathe out long.'"

"Breathing in short, understand, 'I breathe in short.' Breathing out short, understand, 'I breathe out short.'" Attune yourself to the length, movement, feeling, and rhythm of the breath. Stay with the entire breath from start to finish, letting the attention settle little by little.

"Breathe in experiencing the whole body. Breathe out experiencing the whole body."

Once you have established a strong connection with the breath and the attention starts to stabilize, expand the awareness to include the whole body. From here on you will be aware of two things at a time. In this case, you are aware of the breath, and you are aware of the body. This is a delicate balance that requires a careful attention.

"Breathe in calming the body. Breathe out calming the body." You don't so much do the calming yourself, but rather allow the breath to naturally calm and settle the body. Stick with each of these steps until you feel a shift.

Mindfulness of Feeling

"Breathe in experiencing rapture. Breathe out experiencing rapture." Now you are attuning to the pleasant feelings that arise as the mind becomes concentrated and the body becomes tranquil. What you feel might not be as dramatic as "rapture," so just see what feelings arise as you breathe with feelings.

"Breathe in experiencing happiness. Breathe out experiencing happiness." Again, we are just paying attention to whatever feelings are showing up. Whether you call them happiness or not, don't worry. Just relax and enjoy the breath, the body, and the feelings.

"Breathe in experiencing the mental formation. Breathe out experiencing the mental formation." Notice how thoughts are forming even as you try to pay attention to the breath and feelings. Don't follow the thoughts, but stay aware of the tendency of feelings to fuel thought.

"Breathe in calming the mental formation. Breathe out calming the mental formation." As with calming the body, just let this happen naturally. As the attention stabilizes around breath, body, and feelings, a natural calming of thoughts unfolds.

Mindfulness of Mind

"Breathe in experiencing mind. Breathe out experiencing mind." Bring awareness to your state of mind. Calm or busy; grasping or peaceful; irritable or settled. Become aware that everything you experience in your body, feelings, and thoughts is in the mind. As you sit, let the attention expand to include awareness itself, tuning into the subtle experience of pure knowing.

"Breathe in gladdening the mind. Breathe out gladdening the

mind." Enjoy sitting in this space of awareness.

"Breathe in concentrating the mind. Breathe out concentrating the mind." Now make a little more effort to stabilize the attention, resting in the still, open space of mind. The body is calm, the feelings pleasant, the mind quiet.

"Breathe in liberating the mind. Breathe out liberating the mind." Appreciate that the still, concentrated mind has no hindrances. No craving, no aversion, no restlessness. The mind is not caught in any unwholesome activity or states. Sit with and enjoy that.

Mindfulness of Insight

"Breathe in contemplating impermanence. Breathe out contemplating impermanence." Feel how body, feelings, and mind are unstable, constantly changing, in flux. Breathe with that.

"Breathe in contemplating fading away. Breathe out contemplating fading away." Notice how no aspect of body, feelings, thoughts, or mind brings satisfaction. Their instability makes them unsatisfactory.

"Breathe in contemplating cessation. Breathe out contemplating cessation." See that the changing nature of experience is not tied to any stable core or center. The "I" that we ordinarily perceive as having experiences has no substance.

"Breathe in contemplating letting go. Breathe out contemplating letting go." Knowing that the idea of self is empty, let go of clinging to any experience of body or mind.

Gathas

This is a simple breath meditation based on the Anapanasati. It comes from Thich Nhat Hanh and appears in his book *Present Moment, Wonderful Moment*.

For this practice, first establish your posture, with your focus on the breath. Now start to repeat the following phrases silently to yourself with the breath:

In, out
Deep, slow
Calm, ease
Smile, release
Present moment, wonderful moment.

You can do this in one of two ways: either use one phrase per breath, cycling through the phrases. That way, you track five breaths with the five phrases, then start again. The other approach is to use each phrase for several minutes before moving on to the next phrase. Try both and see which one works for you.

Always keep the attention connected to the sensations of breath as you repeat the phrases to yourself.

This is an excellent and easeful concentration practice. You can use it for the entire duration of a meditation period, or for a portion of the sit to get settled.

One note: while you don't want to try to force yourself to feel the things the words are saying, it can be helpful to smile when you get to "smile, release," and to sustain that smile as you practice. Bringing a slight smile to your lips during meditation can have an uplifting effect on the mind. Don't force it, but see if you can integrate this into your practice.

Counting Breaths

Counting breaths is another simple way to calm the mind and develop concentration. There are different ways to do this, and you are free to experiment for yourself. Here is the approach I use:

On the in-breath say to yourself, "in"; on the out-breath say "one." Again, "In," and "two," and so on up to ten. Then go back to one.

If you lose track or the mind wanders, go back to one. Don't try to pick up where you think you got lost. Don't worry if it's hard for you to get to ten. This just shows how busy our minds are.

Metta – Phrases

The practice of Loving Kindness or Metta is meant to cultivate an inner feeling of warmth and love that you can then spread to others. We are trying to awaken a sense of universal caring, unconditional love for all beings, as well as ourselves. Pace this practice according to how much time you are going to do it.

Start by settling the posture and establishing mindfulness of the breath. Put the attention on the "heart center," the area around the chest and solar plexus. Open; relax. Take your time with this, just letting things settle.

Now think of someone who is easy for you to love, a dear person or even a pet. Begin to repeat phrases of loving kindness silently to yourself. You can use your own phrases or these traditional ones:

May you be happy.
May you be peaceful.
May you be safe.

Let the words penetrate your heart. Feel their meaning. Keep an image of the loved one in your mind, stay connected to the breath, and let the words flow. After a few minutes, switch to yourself:

May I be happy.
May I be peaceful.
May I be safe.

Notice any resistance or thoughts that come up. Bring an

attitude of kindness toward these thoughts. Let them go and keep repeating the phrases. Continue to feel the breath and the warmth of kindness in your heart.

Now bring to mind other dear ones, family and friends that you care about. As each person comes to mind, repeat the phrases to yourself:

May you be happy.
May you be peaceful.
May you be safe.

From dear ones, we move to a "neutral" person. This is someone you might encounter in your daily life who isn't important to you and not a problem. It could be someone in a coffee shop you frequent, a neighbor you see, a colleague. Anyone will do as long as you don't feel strongly about them in either a positive or negative way.

May you be happy.
May you be peaceful.
May you be safe.

As you work with the neutral person it can be harder to maintain focus. If the mind wanders, just bring it back to the phrases, the breath, and the image of the person.

Next we work with a difficult person. This can be someone you know, or simply someone you know of like a public figure. Here you may find inner resistance. That's fine. It just gives you insight into the current limits of your capacity for unconditional love. Don't press yourself or judge yourself. Just keep doing the practice with consistency.

May you be happy.
May you be peaceful.
May you be safe.

Lastly, we begin to radiate loving kindness to all beings. Have a sense of loving kindness spreading from your body throughout the building or space you are in; outward to nearby people. Keep expanding your sense of love, letting it flow over cities and countryside; mountains and prairies; oceans and continents.

If so moved, reflect on particular populations that you know need love.

Loving kindness spreads outward into the universe, into space, touching all beings everywhere. Allow the sense of loving kindness to be vast, limitless.

Sit with that feeling of boundlessness. Breathe with that vastness.

Now come back, back into the space you are in, into your body, into your heart, into your breath. See that this limitless loving kindness lives in your own heart, is always available if you simply turn to it.

May all beings be free from suffering.

Metta – Images

(From Buddhist nun Ayya Khema.)

We begin this meditation in the same way, settling the body, connecting with the breath at the heart center, opening and settling.

Now imagine that in your heart there is a beautiful lotus flower with its petals closed. Gradually, as you breathe, the petals peel back, and a golden light shines forth. Feel the golden light shining from the center of your heart.

Let the golden light radiate out and shine on a beloved person. See and feel them being filled with warmth, kindness, and love from the golden light.

Now your beloved reflects the golden light of love back to you, filling you with warmth, kindness, and love. Let your body be suffused with the light of love.

Now let the golden light radiate out to all those you care for, family and friends. See them, one by one, being filled with the light of love radiating from your heart.

Bring to mind neighbors, colleagues, and other "neutral" people, such as people you encounter in shops and cafes. Let the golden light radiate out to them, filling them with warmth, kindness, and love.

Bring to mind a difficult person, someone with whom you've had a conflict or resentment. It doesn't have to be the most difficult person. Let the golden light radiate out to them, filling them with warmth, kindness, and love.

Now begin to radiate the golden light out in all directions, touching everyone in the room; in the building; in the neighborhood. Let the golden light spread throughout your town, touching all the beings: humans, animals, birds, and insects. Let the golden light spread further, across the land and across the sea. All beings are filled with the golden light.

Now the light surrounds and permeates the planet, touching all beings and all things. The earth itself infused with the golden light of loving kindness.

And now let the golden light radiate out into space in all directions. Limitless, unbounded, filling all beings and all things. The entire universe filled with the golden light of loving kindness, radiant, illuminated.

And now, coming back. Coming back to this room, to this body, this heart, to this breath. Bring the golden light back into your heart and let the lotus petals close over it again. See that this limitless loving kindness lives in your own heart, is always there, available to you if you just open to it.

Note: With the practice of radiating Metta/Loving Kindness we can bring our own creativity. Use imagery, phrases, and any other strategies that evoke this feeling and help you to move into this spacious, warm, and caring feeling.

Forgiveness

Forgiveness meditation starts by connecting with the heart:
Begin by settling into a comfortable posture where you can stay alert. Consciously relax with some deeper breaths, releasing any tension in the body.
Feel the breath in the center of the chest, the Heart Center, and have a sense of softening and opening in that place.
Once you've settled in for perhaps 3-5 minutes, begin to work with the following imagery and phrases. The three aspects of forgiveness, forgiving ourselves, forgiving others, and asking forgiveness, can be done in any order that works for you. I present self-forgiveness first because it's so often the most difficult for people.

Forgiving ourselves: begin by contemplating all the ways that you have harmed yourself, internally and externally. This of course includes your addictive behavior, but also ways that you gave up on yourself, whether in school, in a relationship, or in a job. How have you talked to yourself or viewed yourself in negative terms. Self-hatred is a common disease in our culture, especially among addicts, and the truth is, as human beings, we don't deserve to be hated. Repeat these phrases to yourself: For all the ways I have harmed myself through thought, word, and deed, I forgive myself. I forgive myself. We may not feel anything right away, but it's important to stay with this process, and not just in a single sitting, but to keep coming back to this process over time until the tightness in the heart starts to break up and we begin to have a sense of self-forgiveness.

Forgiving others: resentments are sometimes called "the

number one killer" for addicts, and certainly, many of us carry longterm anger, blaming, and trauma. Ultimately, this anger harms us as much as it does our enemy. We are the ones who are living with the nagging thoughts and obsessions. To forgive others does not mean we condone their behavior or that we will ever let them hurt us again. It just means that we don't want to carry this baggage with us. Bring to mind the people who have harmed you and the things they've done to you. Breathing into your heart, say to them, For all the ways you have hurt me through thought, word, or deed, I offer my forgiveness. I forgive you. Again, we can't expect instant results. But we need to stick with this process. Sometimes there will be a sudden shift or insight, and at others just a gradual melting of the icy heart. Stick with it.

Asking Forgiveness: each of us carries a burden of guilt from our addictive and selfish behaviors. Step Nine is about doing something about those unskillful actions. Forgiveness meditation allows us to do the inner work of accepting forgiveness, whether or not we actually receive it externally. For this part of the exercise, think of the people on your Eighth Step list and the ways you harmed each one. Bring each person to mind and say to yourself, For all the ways that I hurt you, through thought, word, or deed, I ask your forgiveness. Please forgive me. Again, it can be difficult to accept that we are forgiven, but this is a form of internal amends, admitting responsibility and asking if we can move on.

Work with these three aspects of forgiveness as much and for as long as is necessary. There's no timetable for forgiveness. You may find that you feel that one of the aspects really stands out as needing attention. That's fine. Use the practice in whatever ways feel beneficial to you.

Other Practices

Buddho – In the Thai Forest Tradition, they use a simple mantra, repeating "Buddho" with the breath. "Bud" on the in-breath and "dho" on the out breath. This is a nice way to settle the mind and stay connected to the breath.

R.A.I.N. - This is a self-guided practice that uses an acronym to remind you to go through a specific process for working with difficult emotions. There are a couple variations on the terms you can use.
R – Recognize – bring mindful awareness to the experience you are having.
A – Accept (Allow) – let go of any resistance to that experience, even if it's unpleasant.
I – Investigate – carefully explore the sensations, feelings, and emotions associated with the experience. Watch the process by which feelings appear and disappear. Here we aren't trying to figure out why it's happening or even put a name on it. Just examine closely what's happening.
N – Non-identify (Nurture) – try not to take what's happening personally. View the experience with equanimity. At the same time bring an attitude of self-compassion to your difficulties.

Appendix I: Buddhist Lists

Four Noble Truths
- The Truth of Suffering: "Birth is suffering, aging is suffering, death is suffering. Not having what you want is suffering; having what you don't want is suffering. In short, the Five Aggregates subject to clinging are suffering." We are supposed to "understand" this truth.
- The Truth of the Cause of Suffering: craving and clinging cause suffering, and this includes aversion. Another way to put this is, "Wanting things to be different from the way they are." We are supposed to "abandon" the cause of suffering, that is, stop clinging, stop craving.
- The Truth of the End of Suffering: when craving ends, suffering ends. This is the goal, to let go of craving. We are supposed to "realize" this truth, that is, to experience the freedom that comes with letting go.
- The Truth of the Way to End Suffering: this is the Noble Eightfold Path. It involves "sila, samadhi, and panna," or morality, mind training (concentration), and wisdom or insight. We are supposed to "develop" the Eightfold Path.

Noble Eightfold Path:
- Right View: seeing the truth of the Four Noble Truths. Understanding the Law of Karma, cause and effect. Fundamentally, Right View is living with wisdom, seeing things as they are, not being deluded.
- Right Intention: being guided by three things: letting go, loving kindness, and compassion. Any thought, word or action should be grounded in one or more of these. We need to look closely at intention because it informs the results of all our actions.

- Right Speech: to speak the truth, in a timely, beneficial manner, and with kindness.
- Right Action: this encompasses the Five Precepts. These are the foundation principles we live by:
  - Not to kill or harm any living beings.
  - Not to steal.
  - Not to do sexual harm.
  - Not to lie.
  - Not to use intoxicants.
- Right Livelihood: using your work and lifeforce for the benefit of others.
- Right Effort: bringing Right Intention to our meditation and other actions. The Middle Way between striving and apathy.
  - Avoiding unwholesome states that aren't present.
  - Letting go of unwholesome states that are present.
  - Cultivating wholesome states that aren't present.
  - Maintaining wholesome states that are present.
- Right Mindfulness:
  - Mindfulness of the Body
  - Mindfulness of Feelings
  - Mindfulness of Mind
  - Mindfulness of Dhammas (the Big Picture)
- Right Concentration: sustained, focused attention. This involves using an "object" of concentration like the breath, a mantra, or image, etc. One continuously returns attention to the object until you are able to stay with it for a sustained period.

Three Characteristics of Existence:
- Impermanence (anicca)
- Suffering/unsatisfactoriness (dukkha)
- Not-self/corelessness (anatta)

Divine Abodes:
- Loving Kindness (metta)
- Compassion (karuna)
- Sympathetic Joy (mudita)
- Equanimity (upekkha)

Five Hindrances:
- Desire
- Aversion
- Sloth and torpor (sleepiness/dullness)
- Restlessness and worry
- Doubt

Seven Factors of Awakening
- Mindfulness
- Investigation of States
- Energy/effort
- Joy
- Tranquility
- Concentration
- Equanimity

Appendix II: The Twelve Steps of Alcoholics Anonymous

1. We admitted we were powerless over alcohol—that our lives had become unmanageable.
2. Came to believe that a Power greater than ourselves could restore us to sanity.
3. Made a decision to turn our will and our lives over to the care of God as we understood Him.
4. Made a searching and fearless moral inventory of ourselves.
5. Admitted to God, to ourselves, and to another human being the exact nature of our wrongs.
6. Were entirely ready to have God remove all these defects of character.
7. Humbly asked Him to remove our shortcomings.
8. Made a list of all persons we had harmed, and became willing to make amends to them all.
9. Made direct amends to such people wherever possible, except when to do so would injure them or others.
10. Continued to take personal inventory and when we were wrong promptly admitted it.
11. Sought through prayer and meditation to improve our conscious contact with God as we understood Him, praying only for knowledge of His will for us and the power to carry that out.
12. Having had a spiritual awakening as the result of these Steps, we tried to carry this message to alcoholics, and to practice these principles in all our affairs.

Appendix III: Buddhist Traditions

When we talk about "Buddhism," just as when we say "Christianity" we are referring to a broad range of traditions and expressions of religious or spiritual teachings and practices. In the broadest sense there are three Buddhist traditions: Theravada, Mahayana, and Vajrayana. The easiest way to fix them in your mind is to connect them with geography. Theravada is the school of Buddhism found in southern and southeastern Asia: Burma, Thailand, and Sri Lanka. (Each of these countries has its own flavor of Theravada.) Mahayana is historically found in China, Korea, Japan, and Vietnam. (Mahayana also is a large umbrella that includes Chan, Pure Land, Son, and Zen among other sects.) Vajrayana is essentially found in the Himalayan countries, Tibet, Nepal, Bhutan, and others. None of this is fixed, and clearly as Buddhism moves to the West, all these schools are found in Europe and North America as well.

Theravada is considered the oldest of these three traditions, tracing its origins back to the historical Buddha and drawing from the earliest texts (suttas) from that era. The other schools evolved over time from this root. Over time certain philosophical and doctrinal disputes triggered various schisms. And perhaps, most importantly, as Buddhism migrated geographically, the cultures of the areas where it arrived had a huge impact on the way the teachings manifested. Thus, the Japanese minimalist aesthetic is expressed in Zen, whereas the colorful Tibetan indigenous religions brought forth the florid quality of Vajrayana.

Each of these traditions developed its own scriptures and meditation practices. Over time they began to look less and less like each other. One thing all three branches of the tradition agree on, however, is the primacy of the Four Noble Truths. The teachings on suffering and the end of suffering are shared across cultures, languages, practices, and scriptures.

My own practice has mostly been guided by Theravada teachings. Mindfulness is most closely associated with this tradition, as the Four Foundations of Mindfulness are central to Theravada Buddhism.

Due to historic forces, the three schools essentially lost touch with each other a thousand years ago. It was only in the nineteenth century as worldwide travel and communication became more common that they started to reconnect. Today, in the West, many people sample from all three schools, choosing not to draw such distinct lines between them.

Resources

Recovery Books:
One Breath at a Time: Buddhism and the Twelve Steps, by Kevin Griffin
Buddhism & the Twelve Steps [series]: by Kevin Griffin
   Workbook
   Daily Contemplations
   Higher Power (Previously published as *A Burning Desire: Dharma God and the Path of Recovery*)
Recovering Joy: A Mindful Life after Addiction, by Kevin Griffin
Eight Step Recovery, by Valerie Mason-John (Vimalasara) and Dr. Paramabandhu Groves
Chi Kung in Recovery, by Greg Pergament
Quit Like a Woman, by Holly Whitaker
Ordinary Recovery, by William Alexander
Recovery Dharma, Anonymous
The Zen Way of Recovery, by Laura Burges
The Mindful Addict, by Tom Catton
A Woman's Way Through the Twelve Steps, by Stephanie Covington
Mindfulness and the 12 Steps, by Therese Jacobs-Stewart

Buddhist Books:
Mindfulness, by Joseph Goldstein
Loving Kindness, by Sharon Salzberg
In the Buddha's Words, by Bhikkhu Bodhi
The Noble Eightfold Path, by Bhikkhu Bodhi
Satipatthana, by Bhikkhu Analayo
A Path with Heart, by Jack Kornfield
A Wise Heart, by Jack Kornfield
Living Kindness, by Kevin Griffin

The Sound of Silence, by Ajahn Sumedho
Being Nature, by Wes Nisker

Websites, Podcasts, Apps:
www.buddhistrecovery.net – Buddhist Recovery Network, resource for meetings, conferences, and teachings.
10% Happier, with Dan Harris, podcast and app
On Being, with Krista Tippett, podcast
Ajahn Amaro, podcast
www.abhayagiri.org – Monastery in the Thai Forest Tradition of Ajahn Chah
www.amaravati.org - Monastery in the Thai Forest Tradition of Ajahn Chah
www.accesstoinsight.org – Suttas
www.suttacentral.org – Suttas
www.buddhistinsightnetwork.org – Insight Meditation community
Insight Timer, app
Head Space, app
Calm, app

Centers:
Spirit Rock Meditation Center
Insight Meditation Society
Southern Dharma Retreat Center
Insight Meditation Center – Redwood City
Insight Meditation Center of Washington
[See https://www.buddhistinsightnetwork.org/ for more Insight Centers]

Monasteries:
Amaravati – England
Abhayagiri – Northern California
Magazines:
Tricycle
Lion's Roar

Acknowledgments

I am the humble and grateful follower of Gautama Buddha, Bill W., and Dr. Bob. The founders of the two traditions, Buddhism and the Twelve Steps, changed the world. They gave me the tools to live the life I've had.

Several friends gave me valuable feedback on an early draft of this book: Ann Bolger Peruzzi, Greg Pergament, Angela Lucia, and Mike Campbell. Walt Opie's deep Dharma knowledge and recovery experience provided vital improvements to the manuscript.

I continue to be inspired and moved by the growth of the Buddhist recovery movement. My own teaching arose out of a wish to share my passion for combining these two paths. It is a great gift to be able to continue to do so.

Thanks to Mike Campbell for his delightful design work. He always demonstrates great patience and generosity in a challenging and tedious process. He is gifted as both an artist and a technician.

Thanks to the recovery teachers who share the seat with me, Vimalasara, Greg Pergament, Ann Bolger Peruzzi, Debbie Darrin, and Walt Opie.

www.ingramcontent.com/pod-product-compliance
Lightning Source LLC
Chambersburg PA
CBHW070159100426
42743CB00013B/2968